recipes to know by heart

♥

Xanthe Clay

recipes to know by heart

Mitchell Beazley

4

Recipes to Know by Heart
Xanthe Clay

An Hachette Livre UK Company
www.hachettelivre.co.uk

First published in Great Britain in 2008 by Mitchell Beazley
An imprint of Octopus Publishing Group Ltd,
2–4 Heron Quays, London E14 4JP
www.octopusbooks.co.uk

ISBN   978 1 84533 358 4
A CIP record for this book is available from the British Library

Commissioning Editor **Rebecca Spry**
Art Director **Tim Foster**
Design & Art Direction **Gabriella Le Grazie**
Deputy Art Editor **Yasia Williams-Leedham**
Photographer **Malou Burger**
Project Editor **Georgina Atsiaris**
Editor **Hattie Ellis**
Production **Sue Fox**
Proofreader **Ruth Baldwin**
Indexer **Diana LeCore**

Set in Akzidenz Grotesk and Berkeley
Printed and bound by Toppan Printing Company, China

contents

INTRODUCTION

This is a book about cooking without a book. That is not as ridiculous as it might sound. Once you have learnt by heart some of the key recipes that follow, kitchen life will become immeasurably simpler. No more scurrying through recipe books for the proportions for a gratin, or pancake batter, or roast beef: it's all in your head.

It will also make shopping easier. We know, because we are always being told so, that we should cook seasonally, shop with an open mind and buy the best of what is available. We should choose the recipe according to those ingredients, rather than match ingredients to a predetermined recipe, with no regard to freshness or quality.

But how can that work, unless you have a bank of recipes in your head? You can buy a perfect satin-skinned butternut squash, then schlep home to find a recipe. Many of us have shelves full of cookbooks, but few of us often have time to scour them for the recipe that fits the ingredients we have. And if we do, we are bound to find we are missing something vital from the ingredients list.

What is the alternative? To trawl through recipe books to find an idea that catches our eye, a fish soup perhaps, then painstakingly write a list, then shop. But what if the fish isn't good that day? Or if the courgettes are so blindingly, perfectly fresh that it would be a crime not to eat them in their prime?

How much better to see the squash and think, shall I make a gratin, or a soufflé, or soup? Or perhaps just roast it? And then to pick up the other necessary items you know are in the recipe – cream, potatoes, eggs, whatever – before heading back to the kitchen to make supper without stress or delay.

And so day-to-day cooking is best done from recipes that we know by heart. Our grandmothers cooked like that, and so do restaurant chefs and the food writers who develop recipes for magazines and newspapers. They know the fundamentals and then adapt these core recipes to make the dish they want.

The recipes in this book are a springboard from which to experiment, have fun and take control in your kitchen. Make a Jerusalem artichoke soufflé without a specific recipe, or a fresh cherry cake, or lamb, lemon and olive casserole: it's easy once you know the grammar of cookery. And once you know the rules, you also know when to break them.

Not that I am pretending that this collection is definitive. Of course there are lots of other ways to make a soup, a soufflé, a casserole. To quote Jane Grigson, they are 'suggestions, not Holy Writ'. And they are a start.

There are 40-odd basic recipes in this book and you may well not want to learn them all. There will be half a dozen – a dozen, even – that are your favourite kind of food to eat. If you learn 15, you'll have enough to see you through a happy culinary life.

This book isn't mine, it's yours. Make it yours. Scribble in the margin the ideas you try out; reminders of combinations you liked and ones that could be improved upon; ideas that you want to have a go at. Make a note of whether you used an extra egg in the soufflé or how much spinach went into the soup so that next time you can build on your experience.

Don't be downcast if things go wrong. One of the charms of cookery, for me, is that it is creative but the results are ephemeral. If the dish isn't as good as you'd hoped, by coffee time you can move on. The next meal will be better. The best way to improve a less successful dish is often to simplify it by using fewer ingredients and fewer competing flavours. Not for nothing is the most often quoted piece of culinary wisdom the chef Escoffier's dictum, '*Faites simple;*' 'Keep it Simple.' This is why the basic recipes in the book have been kept deliberately straightforward.

People sometimes say to me: 'But I never follow a recipe. I just throw in a bit of this, a bit of that. Everyone says I'm a marvellous cook.' It is certainly important to be a sensual cook, to judge by flavour, smell and texture, rather than robotically follow a recipe. But cooking well demands a degree of precision as well as a degree of flexibility. The late, great Elizabeth David, founder and headmistress of modern British cooking, was typically acerbic on the matter. '*Faites simple,*' she said, 'does not mean *faites* slapdash.'

So don't be too cool to weigh ingredients (or, just as good, teach yourself how to measure the right quantity with a spoon or a cup). Chefs often don't measure precisely, it's true, but that is because they have made recipes so often before that they can judge by eye and by feel. The first time they cooked it, believe me, they weighed.

Both metric and imperial measures are included here, since cooks are evenly split between the two. The dual systems can make recipes look cluttered and more complicated than they really are. If it helps, cross out the ones you don't use, or memorize by proportion rather than weight: 1 part sugar to 2 parts butter to 3 parts flour, for roll-and-cut biscuits, say.

Since you must be both scientist and artist in the kitchen – both prescriptive and intuitive – it is vital to concentrate. For the best results, you must be prepared to respond to the raw ingredients. Touch them, smell them, *feel* them. Natural ingredients, fruits, vegetables, meat, are not standardized. The conditions they were grown in, the way they've been stored, the variety, the degree of maturity, all will affect them, and in turn the finished dish. As a cook, it helps to be aware of that.

The parts of cookery which are most scientific and most closely related to chemistry are baking – pastry, bread, biscuits – and also some of the sauces (hollandaise, mayonnaise and so on). Here a reasonable amount of precision is vital. An extra ounce of butter may make the pastry unworkable; an ounce less and it will be dry and dull.

We can be precise about such measurements because flour, butter, sugar and oil are fairly standard. Other recipes – soups and casseroles, for example – rely on ingredients such as meat, fruit and vegetables that vary more. These dishes are more flexible and one can be more relaxed about quantities. Twenty-five per cent more or less of any single ingredient is unlikely to result in disaster.

This leeway also places more responsibility on the cook. No recipe can tell you exactly how much milk to add for the perfect consistency, or exactly how much salt to season with. The water content, starch content and the flavours of the ingredients will vary too much. You, the cook, must be alert to this and be prepared to taste and adjust accordingly.

Think about how your dish tastes, bearing in mind how much you plan to eat. A sauce which will be served by the dollop needs to be more highly seasoned, more assertively flavoured, than a soup which will be eaten by the bowlful. Roll a spoonful around your mouth, concentrate. This way you will train your palate.

Barny Haughton, the pioneering Bristol chef who combines culinary and environmental integrity, speaks with a passionate intensity when he teaches. 'Taste it,' he says, 'and taste with your brain.' He's right, of course. Cooking is fun, but it is more fun if you give it attention and hone your skills, just like skiing or playing tennis, or playing an instrument or painting. Care and concentration will always produce better results than a chuck-it-all-in approach, but intuition and flair play their part, too.

A friend of mine used to garden for Elizabeth David before her death in the 1990s. In her later years she was mostly bed-bound, and he would tell us how she would lie in state, sipping Chablis while watching breakfast television. She hated most television chefs, but one morning a Caribbean cook called Rustie Lee caught her eye. 'That,' she said, 'is food I want to eat.'

Food I want to eat. The phrase has stuck with me ever since. Cooking isn't about impressing people, or following fashion. Nutrition plays a part, but chiefly it's about making food that in some way connects with our subconscious, awakens our appetite. Not food to look at, or admire, or intrigue. Food that begs to be consumed, whose delight is in its taste, texture and to some extent its familiarity and the way it resonates with our past experience. Food you want to eat: that's the point.

Xanthe Clay

MEAT

serves 6–8

3lb 8oz/1.6kg roasting joint of beef,
  pork or lamb
2 tbsp olive oil
salt and pepper

roast beef, pork and lamb

PREPARE THE MEAT. Allow the meat to come to room temperature. Preheat the oven to 230°C/450°F/Gas 8. Weigh the meat and put it on a rack, fat-side up, so the air can circulate around it. Rub the joint with olive oil and season with salt and pepper.

ROAST THE MEAT. Roast for 15 minutes, then reduce the heat to 190°C/375°F/Gas 5. Cook for, per 450g/1lb, 15 minutes for rare, 17 minutes for medium, and 20 minutes for well done. (Pork should not be cooked rare.)

TEST IT'S DONE. Test the meat three-quarters of the way through the cooking time with a meat thermometer or skewer (see pages 13–14) in case it is done early.

REST THE MEAT. When the meat is cooked, let it rest for at least 30 minutes (1 hour is fine) in a warm place, loosely covered by foil or an upturned bowl, before carving.

how to roast a perfect joint

FEW THINGS put more pressure on a cook than roasting meat. First, it would be a shame to ruin a big, expensive joint. And then almost everyone around the table will have rose-tinted memories of the perfect roast of their childhood. To cap it all, there's the expectation of a dozen different accompaniments – vegetables, sauce, gravy, Yorkshire pudding – all of which need careful timing.

Well, to start with, there is absolutely no need to serve more than two vegetables. Gravy is sauce enough (see page 176 for a recipe) and Yorkshire pudding is optional (see page 130). Far, far better to produce a few well-cooked side dishes than get in a spin trying to achieve an impossible number. But, that said, there must be roast potatoes for Sunday lunch.

HOT OR SLOW?

The recipe opposite is for the conventional roast and is the most important one to know. If you have a family group coming, which might include Aunt Mabel (who likes her meat cooked to medium), Cousin Wilfred (a well-done man) and Uncle Brad (who regards anything more than rare as a travesty), the best approach is a traditional roast like this. The relatively high oven temperature will ensure that the outside is well done while the inside remains bloody, so there is plenty of choice (although pork should always be cooked thoroughly, medium-well done).

Amongst my friends, however, who all want it rare (for beef) and rare-to-medium (for lamb), conventional, high-heat roasting will make for a lot of waste or very few who get their meat how they like it. Slow roasting, for a number of hours at a temperature of around 80°C/175°F/Gas ¼, cooks the meat evenly throughout.

There are two minor downsides to slow roasting. The first is that the delicious, savoury, caramelized crust of a classic roast doesn't form on the outside. Get round this by browning the meat well in a pan before it goes in the oven, which also kills any bugs that might be lurking on the surface of the meat. The second is that the gentle heat doesn't force the juices out of the meat, meaning it stays very juicy but there is not much gunk to make gravy with, so you will need to make a sauce or serve some creamy vegetables alongside.

MEAT THERMOMETERS

Short of cutting right into the joint, the only sure-fire way to check the doneness of the meat is with a meat thermometer. There are plenty available. The simplest are no more than a dial on a spike and the best ones have a probe that stays in the meat throughout roasting and a digital screen that sticks magnetically to the oven-front. There's an alarm which can be set to go off when the meat reaches the right temperature.

One caveat. Some of the thermometers have preset indicators for rare, medium and well done. While these temperatures are perfectly correct, the meat needs to be removed from the oven when it is a good 10°C/18°F cooler for the hot-roast method, or 5°C/9°F cooler for the slow-roast method. As the meat rests, heat on the surface will travel into the centre, the temperature will rise significantly and the meat will keep cooking.

THE SKEWER TEST

Less accurate than a thermometer, but still effective, is the skewer test. Stick the skewer into the meat at the thickest part, but without the tip touching the bone. Leave for 30 seconds. Pull it out and touch the tip to your lip, or the inside of your wrist, and assess the heat. Cold – raw; tepid – rare; warm – medium; hot – well done. Look at the colour of the juices that leak out as well. Red means rare, pink medium and clear or brown means well done.

HOW MUCH TO BUY

Estimating quantities is always tricky since people's appetite for meat varies enormously, and a good carver can make the joint go further. As a rough guide, allow a generous 280g/10oz per person for meat on the bone and 200g/7oz per person for meat off the bone, plus a bit extra for sandwiches the next day.

PORK

Pork should be cooked medium-well done, to an internal temperature of 75°C/167°F, to kill the parasite trichinella. This nematode is extremely rare in farmed pigs, but the infection it causes can be nasty enough to want to rule out any risk. In omnivorous or carnivorous wild animals it is much more common. In Ohio a few years ago there was an outbreak after bear meat was served at a church supper, so, should the occasion arise, I'll be having my bear steak well done.

timings for a perfect joint

SLOW ROASTING

Preheat the oven to 80°C/175°F/Gas ¼. Heat a tablespoon of oil over a high heat in a frying pan and cook the meat on all sides until it's a good hazelnut-brown (10–15 minutes). Transfer the meat to the oven and roast until it has reached the correct internal temperature, which will take around 2½ hours to come to rare. The timings may seem impossibly vague, but meat cooked this way can 'hold' for 2 hours or more. If the internal temperature threatens to get too high, just take the meat out of the oven, tent loosely with foil

TEMPERATURES FOR SLOW ROASTING

Stick the thermometer into the meat at the thickest part, but without the tip of the probe touching the bone.

rare	50–55°C/122–131°F, rising to 60°C/140°F after resting
medium	60–65°C/140–149°F, rising to 70°C/158°F after resting
well done	70–75°C/158–167°F, rising to 80°C/176°F after resting

and keep it in a warm place out of draughts. Start it off 3½ hours before you plan to eat, and keep it resting while you cook the vegetables, secure in the knowledge that the meat is already done to perfection.

FACTORS THAT CAN CAUSE VARIATION IN THE COOKING TIME

A number of factors can affect the cooking time: density in the grain of the meat; the temperature of the meat when it goes in the oven; variations in oven temperature; and other dishes being cooked in the oven at the same time.

For this reason, ALWAYS double check with a thermometer or the skewer test three-quarters of the way through the cooking time, or after 1½ hours for slow cooking, and take the meat out of the oven as soon as it reaches the internal temperature you are looking for, regardless of how long it has been in the oven.

HOT ROASTING

Timings can only ever be approximate, since a lot depends on the shape, as well as the weight of the meat. A long, thin fillet of beef will cook more quickly than a chunk of sirloin that's as thick as it is long. (If you are lucky enough to have a whole beef fillet, roast it at 220°C/425°F/Gas 7 for 25 minutes for rare, 30 minutes for well done.)

TEMPERATURES FOR HOT ROASTING

The rule of thumb for how long to roast a fairly chunky cut is:

- start with: 15 minutes at 230°C/450°F/Gas 8

- reduce the heat to: 180°C/350°F/Gas 4

- followed by (per 450g/1lb):

rare	15 minutes
medium	17 minutes
well done	20 minutes

- to get an internal temperature of:

rare	52°C/125°F, rising to 60°C/140°F as it rests
medium	60°C/140°F, rising to 70°C/158°F as it rests
well done	70°C/158°F, rising to 80°C/176°F as it rests

good roasts to make

Roast leg of lamb with anchovies on tomato and potato gratin ➥

A gorgeous all-in-one dish that makes a good summer dinner. The anchovies give a richly savoury flavour that is not at all fishy.

Preheat the oven to 230°C/450°F/Gas 8. Spike a leg of lamb (bone-in, weighing about 3kg/6½lb) in eight or ten places, making slits about 2cm/¾in deep. Cut 2 anchovies from a 50g/1¾oz tin into four long pieces and push a piece into each slit, along with a shard of garlic (you'll need about a clove in total). Rub the whole joint with a little olive oil and a good pinch of salt.

Peel and thinly slice 1.5kg/3lb potatoes and put in a large bowl with the rest of the tin of anchovies and their oil, 4 fat cloves of garlic, crushed, and the leaves from a few sprigs of thyme. Toss together, adding enough olive oil so that everything feels well lubricated, and plenty of salt and pepper. Tip into a large baking dish (about 35x20cm/14x8in). Arrange 450g/1lb sliced tomatoes over the top and pour over a large glass of wine (140ml/5fl oz) and a little oil. Put the lamb on a rack over the vegetables.

Roast for 15 minutes, then reduce the temperature to 180°C/350°F/Gas 4. Cook for about 1½ hours for rare lamb (1¾ hours for medium and 2 hours for well done), basting occasionally with juices from the potatoes. Check with a skewer or thermometer three-quarters of the way through cooking.

Take the lamb out of the oven and keep in a warm place, covered loosely in foil. Assess the potatoes, giving them a bit longer in the oven if they seem underdone or too liquid. Otherwise just keep them warm in a low oven (about 80°C/175°F/Gas ¼).

Pour over the potatoes any juices that come out of the lamb as it rests. Serve slices of the lamb with the potato gratin and some green beans or watercress. Serves 10.

Slow-roast beef with beetroot purée and horseradish crème

This buttery beetroot purée does double duty as vegetable and sauce, and can be made in advance and reheated in a pan or the microwave. Topside is cheaper but not as tender as sirloin, so if you are using the former it needs to be top quality and carved in thin slices.

Preheat the oven to 80°C/175°F/Gas ¼ and put a roasting tin in the oven to heat up. Rub a 900g/2lb piece of rolled sirloin or topside with olive oil and season.

Heat a heavy frying pan until hot. Brown the meat on all sides (up to 10 minutes). Put the meat in the hot roasting tin and cook for 3 hours or until a meat thermometer reads 50–55°C/122–131°F. It will keep warm for an hour in a turned-off oven.

Meanwhile, blitz 450g/1lb cooked beetroot (vac-pac is fine, so long as it has no vinegar) in a food processor until smooth. Peel 450g/1lb potatoes. Cook them in well-salted water, drain well and mash with 55g/2oz butter, then mix with the beetroot. Taste and season, adding more butter if necessary. Mix 2 tbsp hot horseradish sauce into a small tub of crème fraîche.

Slice the meat and serve with the beetroot purée, horseradish crème and a posy of fresh watercress. Serves 4–5.

serves 4

1 chicken (about 3lb 8oz/1.6kg)

olive oil

salt and pepper

2 medium onions, peeled and halved

4 large carrots, peeled

roast chicken

PREPARE THE CHICKEN. Take the chicken out of the fridge about an hour before cooking. Preheat the oven to 200°C/400°F/Gas 6. Pull out any gobbets of fat from inside the bird, and also the bag of giblets if there is one (there hardly ever is nowadays). Rub the outside with olive oil, concentrating on the breast. Season inside and out with salt and pepper.

ROAST ON A RACK OF VEGETABLES. Lay the onions and carrots over the base of a roasting tin. Sit the chicken on top. Roast for about an hour, basting when you have a chance. Check that it's cooked through by spearing the fattest part of the thigh with a skewer: if the juices are pink, give it another 10–15 minutes in the oven and check again.

REST THE CHICKEN BEFORE CARVING. Leave to rest in a warm place, covered loosely in foil or under a large upturned mixing bowl, for at least 20 minutes, and up to an hour, before carving.

how to make perfect roast chicken

THE BIRD

A decent chicken is the starting point. Best of all, buy from a farm (ideally one you've visited) where you know that the welfare standards are high and the chickens have decent-quality feed, are not given prophylactic medication and live for 11 weeks or so rather than the standard 6 weeks. Older birds have a better flavour, as do properly fed ones, and who wants to eat an unhappy chicken?

For those of us without that inside track, buying from a butcher we trust is a good second best. Even at the supermarket, we can look for free-range birds, or at least Freedom Food chickens, which are reared to respectable standards monitored by the RSPCA.

Organic certification on a chicken translates to the highest standards of all, especially if they are Soil Association certified, the most rigorous and reliable of the organic certifications. But bear in mind that not every farmer chooses to go the organic route, and the very best of the 'conventional' farms probably exceed some of the organic farms in terms of welfare and quality.

THE VEGETABLES

Put the vegetables below the chicken in order to give the gravy more flavour (see page 176).

COOKING FROM ROOM TEMPERATURE

Taking the chicken out of the fridge a good hour before it needs to go in the oven means it cooks evenly and as quickly as possible.

CRISP SKIN

Rubbing the skin with salt and oil before the bird goes in the oven will make for crisper skin.

TO TRUSS OR NOT TO TRUSS?

Trussing the bird (tying the legs together tightly) is said to protect the breast and keep it moist. But it also compacts the meat and makes it harder for the heat to travel, increasing cooking time. I find it far better to roast the chicken quickly, untrussed.

TOPSY-TURVY

Some cooks favour roasting the bird upside down, or first on one breast, then on the other. I think the idea is to redistribute the juices more evenly and keep the breast meat juicy. That's fine, but I'm yet to be convinced of the benefits. Stuffing under the skin, however, is a sure-fire way to keep the bird moist and full of flavour.

STUFFING BENEATH THE SKIN

Stuffing the cavity of the bird is not a great idea, since the weight of the stuffing must be calculated into the cooking time and a longer cooking time means there is a greater chance of the bird drying out. Far better to insert a small amount of highly flavoured, buttery (or otherwise fatty) stuffing under the breast skin, protecting it from overcooking whilst flavouring and basting the meat at the same time.

good things to slip under the skin of a roast chicken

TO INSERT STUFFING underneath the skin of the bird, you'll need to loosen the skin over the breast first. It's a bit fiddly but not difficult. Undo the trussing on the chicken and sit it with the legs pointing towards you. Ease your fingers under the breast skin, breaking any membranes holding the skin to the meat. Try hard not to break the skin. If you do, skewer it together with a cocktail stick, or perfectionists can to sew it up with a needle and thread. Now slip your stuffing into this envelope you've created, carrying it right over the legs if you can.

Dried mushrooms Soak 15g/½oz dried porcini mushrooms in boiling water. Chop the mushrooms and mix with 55g/2oz butter. Save the soaking water to add to the gravy.

Streaky bacon Take 4 rashers of streaky bacon, smoked is best, halve them crossways and slip them under the skin, laying them as flat as possible. Push in 2 whole rosemary sprigs as well.

Goat's cheese Mash about 90g/3oz soft goat's cheese with the leaves from 4 sprigs of fresh thyme.

Tarragon Strip the leaves from a small bunch of fresh tarragon, chop them and mix with 55g/2oz butter and the juice of a lemon.

Fresh 'wet' garlic When it comes into season in spring, mash 3–4 cloves of fresh garlic with 55g/2oz butter and a chopped small bunch of flat leaf parsley. This is good with standard garlic too (but use less as it is stronger).

Harissa Deseed 3 large red chillies and grill them, skin-side up, until blackened. Purée, skin and all, in the food processor with half a grilled, peeled and deseeded red pepper. Add a pinch of ground cumin, another of salt and 1 tsp rosewater if you have it, then mix in 2 tbsp olive oil. Squelch this sloppy mixture under the skin of the chicken. In a hurry? Belazu rose harissa is so good I hardly ever make my own. Use it just as it is, straight from the jar.

serves 1

1 sirloin steak (about 5–7oz/150–200g)
  cut 1¼in/3cm thick

1 tbsp black peppercorns, crushed in a pestle
  and mortar

1 tsp butter (unsalted is best)

salt

2 tbsp brandy

2 tbsp red wine

4 tbsp whipping cream

steak au poivre

PEPPER THE STEAK. Press the peppercorns into both sides of the steak. Leave to come up to room temperature.

HEAT THE PAN AND FRY THE STEAK. Heat the butter in a frying pan over a medium-high heat. When it is foaming, sprinkle the steak with salt and cook for 2½ minutes on each side (add a minute on each side if you prefer your steak medium-rare, 2 minutes for medium).

FLAME THE BRANDY. Tip the brandy into the hot pan, allowing it to bubble up. Hold a lighted match to the pan – stand back! When the flames subside, take out the steak and keep in a warm place.

STIR IN THE WINE, letting it bubble up, stirring and scraping to get all those yummy, sticky, caramelized meat juices mixed in.

STIR IN THE CREAM and bubble gently until thickened. Spoon the sauce over the steak. Serve with chips or mashed potatoes.

how to cook the perfect steak

A STEAK SUPPER is certainly simple, but not necessarily easy. It takes care to get each steak nicely browned on the outside and also done inside to each person's liking. Practice, as with so many things, quickly makes perfect, so even if it's not exactly right the first time, at least you've got a good excuse to have steak again another night.

THE STEAK

First things first. The steak itself must be good. It should be fillet or sirloin, or possibly, if it's from a really good butcher, rump or goose skirt, although both these must be cooked rare and sliced fairly thinly before being arranged on a plate.

Choose steak that has a good, deep brown-red colour, like an aged claret. There should be a good marbling of creamy-coloured (not bright white) fat. The best will have been dry-aged on the bone for 21 days or more.

The steak needs to be really dry if it is to brown properly, so press a piece of kitchen towel on to the surface. It also needs to be at room temperature, so give it an hour or so out of the fridge before cooking, or pick up the steak on the way home for an after-work treat and cook it straight from the shopping bag.

TIMINGS

The timings for cooking steak are approximate, since it is impossible to be exact. Test for doneness by pressing the steak with your finger. Try first with the raw steak: it will feel soft like a soft pillow. When rare, it will feel bouncier, more like a soft mattress. Medium is springy like a firmer mattress and well done has very little give at all. This method takes practice, but start now and in a few steaks' time you'll be a pro. When frying, let the steak be for a couple of minutes before trying to move it so it can brown properly.

RESTING

Eating steak straight out of the pan would be like drinking tea before it's brewed. It needs to rest for a good 5 minutes (and 15 won't do any harm). Although no heat is being applied, you should count this as part of the cooking time.

A PAN SAUCE

The liquid could be stock or alcohol – brandy or wine, say, in which case it's important it boils right down to get rid of the alcohol which gives a raw taste. Flambéing the alcohol – holding a match to the pan so that the alcohol vapour ignites – reduces the sharpness that booze tends to give the sauce. It's also quite fun and not dangerous.

If the sauce is still a bit sharp, butter or cream will soften the flavours, as well as giving a rich unctuousness. Beat in dice of cold butter one at a time over a gentle heat to thicken the sauce a little. Or add cream, letting it bubble up and thicken.

good things to eat with steak

STEAK WITH MIXED PEPPERCORNS

Rather than just black pepper (delicious though it is), green or any mix of peppercorns can be used in a steak au poivre. Look out for the special single-variety ones in supermarkets and delis. I like to finish the dish with ½ tsp fruity green peppercorns or aromatic pink peppercorns, which aren't really peppercorns at all, but have a delicious resinous flavour nonetheless.

STEAK WITH MUSHROOMS

Slice 55g/2oz mushrooms (wild or cultivated) and fry in butter. Deglaze the steak pan with a small wineglassful (about 100ml/4fl oz) red wine or marsala, and tip the deglaçage into the mushroom pan. Heat through, adding enough stock or cream to get the right consistency for a sauce.

CHIPS

Deep-frying isn't in my daily repertoire, but I'll happily make an oven-baked version of chips. Peel 1 medium potato per person and cut into medium-sized chips (about 1–1½cm/½in thick). Toss them in oil and a pinch of salt. Lay them in a well-spaced single layer on non-stick baking parchment and bake for 30 minutes at 200°C/400°F/Gas 6, turning halfway through.

Steak with pink peppercorns, parsley and anchovy ➡

Mild tasting pink peppercorns (actually a dried berry) are particularly good with steak. Anchovy adds a savoury depth of flavour, without making the sauce remotely fishy.

Heat 1 tsp unsalted butter in a frying pan over a medium-high heat. When it is foaming, sprinkle 2 sirloin steaks (about 150–200g/5–7oz each in weight, 3cm/1¼in thick) with salt and cook for 2½ minutes on each side (add a minute on each side if you prefer your steak medium-rare, 2 minutes for medium). Put the steaks on a warmed plate and keep to one side, out of draughts.

Tip 2 tbsp brandy into the hot pan, and hold a match to it so it flames up. When the flames subside, add 3 chopped anchovies and stir vigorously so that they dissolve into the sauce. Add 2 tbsp wine, letting it bubble up for a minute or so, still stirring. Now stir in 4 tbsp crème fraîche, 1 tbsp roughly chopped flat-leaf parsley and 1 tsp pink peppercorns, plus any juices that have accumulated under the steaks, and bubble gently until thickened.

Spoon the sauce over the steaks. Serve with chips or mashed potatoes. Serves 2.

serves 2

8oz/225g tender beef, pork or chicken (fillet or breast)

1 tbsp oil

1 clove of garlic, sliced/1 olive-sized piece of fresh
ginger, sliced/1 mild chilli, deseeded and sliced

a handful of cashew nuts (optional)

8oz/225g sliced vegetables cut into
similar-sized pieces

for the sauce:

1 tbsp soy sauce

1 tsp cornflour

1 tbsp grated fresh ginger

4 tbsp water

2 tbsp Chinese rice wine or sherry (optional)

stir-fry

PREPARE THE INGREDIENTS. Cut the meat into thin slices that are roughly the same size and mix the sauce ingredients together.

HEAT THE PAN over a high heat for at least a minute, then pour in the oil, swirling it round so that it coats the sides.

FLAVOUR THE OIL IN THE PAN by adding the garlic/ginger/chilli (one, two or all, according to taste). Lower the heat a little and cook until they begin to colour. Scoop out the flavourings and bin them – they have done their job.

ADD THE NUTS, if you're using them, stirring them round over a high heat until they are browned. Scoop them out with a slotted spoon and put in a bowl.

ADD THE MEAT. Spread the meat in a single layer in the pan and leave without stirring for a minute or two to get some colour, then turn, brown again and scoop out into the bowl with the nuts.

ADD THE VEGETABLES. Add more oil to the pan if necessary, then tip in the vegetables one type at a time, starting with those which need the longest cooking, such as carrots and onions, and finishing with the leafy veg.

HEAT EVERYTHING THROUGH WITH THE SAUCE. Return the meat and nuts to the pan and stir and toss vigorously over a high heat. Pour the sauce into the pan. Heat through, adding more water if necessary, and then serve straight away.

what you need to make a stir-fry

I FIND IT HELPS to have a simple default formula stir-fry for those times when I long for a healthy, vegetable-rich supper. This recipe is not especially authentic, but it hits the right buttons – salty, savoury, spicy – and is a good base for adding other flavourings.

THE INGREDIENTS

Resist the temptation to use a stir-fry to clear out the fridge. It is a good vehicle for the odd single red pepper or half bunch of spring onions, but use too many different ingredients and it'll end up looking and tasting like a jumbled mess. Stick to a maximum of four main ingredients.

THE SAUCE

There are any number of combinations and recipes to try, but it helps to have a failsafe combination in your head. Soy, fresh root ginger and garlic are the main flavourings. Ginger root dries out quickly, so if you don't use it all that much, keep it in the freezer and grate as much as you need straight from frozen. Invest in some decent soy sauce, which has more flavour and less salt. Clearspring and Kikkoman are both good brands. A splash of Chinese rice wine (available from most supermarkets) adds authenticity, or use dry sherry.

THE WOK

You want a pan that responds quickly when the burner is adjusted. Heavy cast-iron ones aren't just expensive, they are slow to heat up and slower to cool, and ones with non-stick coating can't withstand the high temperatures. Choose a carbon steel wok – a cheap one from a Chinese supermarket is fine. It should have a curved, not flat, base, so everything can be swirled around easily and just a small amount of oil is needed.

Season the wok to give it a natural non-stick surface. Wash it well with hot soapy water, dry it and smear the inside with vegetable oil (not olive oil). Heat until the wok starts to smoke, then allow it to cool. Rub well with kitchen paper, to remove the blackened oil. Repeat the oiling, heating and wiping twice more before using the wok to cook: it'll darken to brown or black.

After cooking, never use detergent on the wok or put it in the dishwasher. Rinse it with hot water, then wipe it out with kitchen paper and rub with a tiny bit of oil. Use oil and salt to scrub it lightly to remove any cooked-on food. Treated like this, the wok's surface will improve with age, and the food will taste better each time.

THE STARCH

Boiled rice is the obvious accompaniment (100g/4oz per person), or add noodles to the mix. Those ready-cooked noodles in sachets are stodgy and weird-tasting, so stick to dried egg, rice or udon noodles. Preboil them according to the packet instructions (about 55g/2oz person), then cool them under a cold tap, drain and toss with a teaspoon of sesame oil: hot, wet noodles tend to stick in the wok.

how to make a perfect stir-fry

STIR FRYING MAKES a good supper for one or two, three at a pinch. Don't try to cook for more or the wok will be overloaded and the food will steam in its own juices instead of frying.

PREPARATION
Once you've started cooking, there is no time to stop and chop, so get everything prepared before you heat the wok. Cut the vegetables and meat into equal-sized slivers, and put into separate bowls ready to be tipped into the pan.

HEATING THE WOK AND THE OIL
Always heat the wok before adding the oil. As for which oil to use, groundnut or grapeseed are best but sunflower oil will do. Trickle it in around the edge to coat the surface evenly. And keep that heat high, to get the proper smoky flavour.

THE VEGETABLES
If you aren't confident of the cooking times, stir-fry the vegetables one after another, keeping the cooked ones to one side. The disadvantage is that this method will probably need more oil and the finished dish will be fattier. Otherwise follow the order given in the box below.

THE COOKING ORDER

The order in which the ingredients are added is important, since those that need the longest cooking time should be added first. As a rough guide:
1. Flavourings for the oil such as garlic, chilli, sliced ginger (scoop out and bin once browned)
2. Nuts (scoop out and set aside)
3. Meat (scoop out and set aside)
4. Root vegetables (carrots, onions, turnips, parsnips), all thinly sliced to speed the cooking. Aubergine also needs to go in early, since undercooked it's inedible.
5. Medium-textured vegetables and sturdy leaves (broccoli, mushrooms, peppers, bok choy stems, cabbage)
6. Tender leaves (spinach, bok choy leaves, Chinese cabbage)
7. Cooked meat and nuts (see 2 and 3 above)
8. Sauce ingredients
9. Herbs and sesame oil

STIRRING
Hold back from stirring the meat, which needs time undisturbed to colour. But vegetables need stirring all the time to cook evenly. Tossing the contents of the pan like a TV chef is optional and no harder than flipping a pancake. Practise with a ziplock bag half full of dried beans. You'll be out-Ainsley-ing Ainsley in no time.

good things to add to stir-fries

NUTS
Cashew nuts are good with prawns, tofu, beef and other meat and fish as well as with chicken. Other good nuts include almonds and peanuts. They add protein as well as flavour and texture to vegetarian stir-fries.

SESAME SEEDS AND OIL
A couple of tablespoonfuls of sesame seeds, lightly toasted and sprinkled over at the end of cooking, works well with pork and chicken. Sesame oil should be sprinkled over at the end as a flavouring, as it burns too easily to use for frying. Choose toasted sesame oil for the most intense flavour, and use sparingly. It's especially good with tofu and aubergine stir-fries. And do store sesame oil in the fridge, since like nut oils it goes rancid quickly.

CITRUS ZEST
Take off strips of zest with a zester and let them dry by laying them on a plate and leaving uncovered overnight. Crumble the brittle shreds or grind them to a powder in a pestle and mortar and store them in an airtight container for up to a month. Add a generous pinch to stir-fries. Lemon is particularly good with fish and chicken, and orange works well with pork or beef.

CHINESE FIVE SPICE POWDER
This blend of spices (star anise, fennel, cloves, cinnamon and Szechuan pepper all usually feature) is particularly good with beef and duck. Mix a teaspoonful into the sauce or sprinkle it over just after adding the vegetables and stir everything together.

SOFT HERBS
Some herbs, such as coriander and basil, are good with all stir-fries. Scatter them over generously at the end, to keep them lively. Look out for Thai basil, with its distinctive aniseed flavour. It gives an authentic flavour to Thai stir-fries.

Mint is good in moderation for south-east Asian flavour, especially with a finely sliced lemongrass stalk (throw away the tough outer leaves first), a sliced chilli and a teaspoonful of brown sugar added to the sauce.

Chives, especially garlic chives, are really lovely with prawns.

SAUCES
These vary enormously from brand to brand, but as a rough guide:
❧ Black bean sauce: rich and dark, like a heavily reduced beef stock. Use with meat stir-fries.
❧ Oyster sauce: salty and reminiscent of anchovy sauce. Good in most dishes.
❧ Hoisin sauce: a smoky, barbecue sauce flavour, especially good with red meat and duck.
❧ Yellow bean sauce: milder and fruitier than black bean sauce. Try it with white meat and fish.

a good stir-fry to make

Chicken, broccoli and almond stir-fry ➤

Simple and satisfying, this makes the perfect after-work supper.

Mix the sauce ingredients together: 1 tbsp soy sauce, 1 tbsp grated fresh ginger, 2 tbsp dry sherry or Chinese rice wine, 1 tsp cornflour and 4 tbsp water. Keep to one side.

Slice a skinned chicken breast thinly, across the grain. Slice 4 spring onions on the diagonal. Cut a head of broccoli into small florets. If you want to have some heat, slice a medium red chilli into thin rings, taking out the seeds first or not, depending on how hot you want the stir-fry.

Heat the wok or a large frying pan, then add 1 tbsp oil and heat until almost smoking. Stir in 2 sliced cloves of garlic, heating them until golden brown, then scoop them out and throw away.

Add a handful of blanched almonds, cook until pale gold, then scoop out and keep to one side.

Spread the sliced chicken out in the wok, allow to sizzle for a few seconds, then toss until lightly coloured and cooked through. Scoop out the meat and set aside.

Add the spring onion and chilli (if using) to the pan, plus a little more oil if necessary. Cook, stirring, for 1 minute, then tip in the broccoli and stir for another minute, until just cooked.

Return the cooked chicken and nuts to the wok. Add the sauce and heat through, stirring and tossing, adding a little more water if necessary. Serves 2 people, with rice or noodles.

serves 4–6

1 onion, peeled and sliced

3 tbsp olive oil

1–2 tbsp flour

salt and pepper

1–2lb/450g–900g meat, cut into ¾in/2cm
  cubes, or chicken portions

½ bottle of red wine (or white for a delicate
  pork or chicken casserole)

stock or water

a sprig of parsley

a sprig of thyme or rosemary

a simple casserole

COOK THE ONION in 2 tbsp of the olive oil in a large saucepan or flameproof casserole until soft and translucent. Scoop out of the pan and keep to one side.

PREPARE THE MEAT. Season the flour with a good pinch of salt and a grind of pepper and toss the meat in it. Add the remaining oil to the pan and heat to medium-hot.

FRY THE MEAT, half a dozen pieces at a time, over a medium-high heat until well browned on all sides.

SPLASH IN THE WINE and let it bubble up, stirring all the time. Return all the meat and the onion to the pan, adding a little stock or water so that the meat is more or less submerged. Tuck in the herbs. Season.

SIMMER, covered, for at least 45 minutes or until the meat is tender (most casseroles take about 1½ hours). Taste and adjust the seasoning.

what you need to make a casserole

A WARMING CASSEROLE should consist of meltingly tender meat in a richly flavoured sauce that begs to be mopped up with good bread or squidged into mashed potato. The key is careful softening of the onion and proper browning of the meat, followed by gentle, lengthy cooking. Most casseroles are also improved by an overnight rest in the fridge, before reheating the following day. This also gives the opportunity to lift off any excess fat that has risen to the surface and set.

THE MEAT

First things first. Any meat can be braised or stewed, but it needs to be a muscular piece with plenty of connective tissue or else it will be stringy and disappointing. So beef fillet is out, as is chicken breast – at any rate, if it's from a modern, mollycoddled bird. You need a proper free-range or organic chicken for a good stew. This is partly because the meat has built up flavour and texture, and partly because the bones have calcified enough to give texture to the juices.

If I'm honest, it's the fullest-flavoured meats – beef, lamb and venison – that make the best casseroles. Pork, veal and chicken need plenty of help if they are not to be insipid, so bring on the spices, the prunes and the herbs.

GOOD CUTS FOR CASSEROLES

Beef: shin, leg, brisket, chuck, neck and blade. Simmer for 2 hours or so, except oxtail which takes up to 4 hours.

Pork: most leaner cuts work well but you can use very fatty cuts like belly cut into small pieces to enrich the casserole. Simmer for about 1½ hours.

Lamb and mutton: shanks, scrag, middle neck, shoulder and chump. Belly of lamb is too fatty to work well, and while leg will work, it is relatively expensive. Simmer for 1½–2 hours.

Chicken and other poultry: leg and wing are better than breast. The skin can make the dish very fatty and has a floppy texture, so I often pull it off and throw it away before browning the meat. Simmer for 45 minutes or so.

THIS LITTLE PIGGY…

If you can get a pig's trotter – and I know it's not the sort of thing one often finds in Tesco – add it to the pot. You can always fish it out before serving, so it needn't scare the family, but it will give a tremendous gloopy texture to the stew. Buy pig's trotters from enlightened butchers (and, even then, they are unlikely to be on display, so ask for them). If you are buying other meat, they may not even charge you. Give the trotters a good scrub and trim off the hornier bits of toenail, then freeze each one in its own bag. Defrost when needed and toss whole into the simmering pan.

how to make a perfect casserole

SOFTENING THE ONION

To do the initial frying, use a casserole dish that can go on the hob or a wide, shallow pan like a sauté pan. Cook the vegetables for 10 minutes or more, until really soft and translucent: there should be no crunch. A little browning will do no harm. Adding a crushed clove of garlic for the last minute or so is also a good idea and you can use leek or shallots instead of onion. Some chopped bacon, cooked with the vegetables, is a good addition – use a couple of rashers per 450g/1lb meat.

BROWNING THE MEAT

Not everyone tosses the meat in flour (use 1 tbsp per 450g/1lb meat), but it helps the meat to brown nicely and thickens the sauce. Heat the oil to medium-hot (not smoking) and throw in half a dozen cubes of meat. Prod them gingerly after a couple of minutes: if they release themselves easily from the base of the pan they are ready to turn. Cook on all sides (well, at least four of the six sides) until well browned, by which I mean a good, hazelnut-shell colour, not the greyish beige of steamed meat. Transfer the meat to a bowl, splash a little water into the pan and stir vigorously to scrape up the residue. Add this liquid to the bowl. Fry the rest of the meat in the same way, using a little more oil each time. This takes time and patience, but you can read the paper as you go.

BOILING THE ALCOHOL

Pour a half bottle of wine (or the equivalent amount of stout, about 375ml/13fl oz) into the now empty pan and bring to the boil. If you want, you can also put a lighted match to the surface of the liquid to ignite the alcohol fumes. This reduces the acidity of the sauce (and is fun in a theatrical way). Simmer for 3 minutes or so.

SIMMERING THE CASSEROLE

If you do the initial cooking in a frying pan (it can be quicker and easier), now turn the meat into a deep casserole or pot. Make sure the meat is pretty much covered in liquid (add a little water or stock if necessary). Cover with a well-fitting lid and simmer very gently, stirring occasionally, until the meat is tender. Don't let it boil. There should be just the odd lazy bubble appearing on the surface. If it is seething like a Jacuzzi, the meat will tighten and toughen. This should take about 45 minutes to 2 hours, depending on how tender the meat was to start with: chicken joints rarely need longer than an hour, but some stewing steak, full of connective tissue, could take 2 hours or more.

Don't overcook the meat or it can become woolly and dull. If the juices seem too thin and plentiful, scoop out the meat before boiling down the liquid to thicken it. Return the meat to the pan and gently heat through again.

good things to add to a casserole

BEEF CASSEROLES
❥ Red wine, stout or beer.
❥ A strip of orange zest or a whole star anise with the herbs.
❥ A plum-sized chunk of black pudding, chopped into small pieces.
❥ A generous handful (around 225g/8oz) of tiny pickling onions, peeled and fried until golden, instead of the chopped onion.
❥ 225g/8oz stubby sticks of carrot the size of a Fox's Glacier Mint.
❥ A squeeze of tomato purée.
❥ 4 or so rashers of bacon, smoked or not, cut into strips and fried with the onion.

LAMB CASSEROLES
❥ Red or rosé wine, unless it's pale milk-fed spring lamb, in which case brown the meat only lightly, and use white wine and 150ml/5fl oz double cream or crème fraîche.
❥ A 400g/13oz can each of cooked flageolet beans and tomatoes.
❥ A fat pinch of saffron strands and a shake of chilli powder.
❥ A small handful of dried apricots or prunes is very good with saffron and chilli as above, or with a cinnamon stick tucked in to infuse as the casserole simmers.

CHICKEN CASSEROLES
❥ A bunch of tarragon: add the stalks with the wine and the chopped leaves for the last 10 minutes or so.
❥ Sherry, red wine or white wine.
❥ 140g/5oz sliced mushrooms, fried with the onion.

VENISON CASSEROLES
❥ Gutsy red wine.
❥ A square or two of dark chocolate, 70 per cent cocoa solids.
❥ Around 140g/5oz sliced mushrooms, especially wild mushrooms or 25g/1oz dried porcini soaked in hot water (add the soaking water too, straining out the grit first).

a good casserole

Oxtail osso buco ◄

A classic osso buco is made with veal, but this darker version is deliciously unctuous. The magic ingredients are the black pudding, which melts into the sauce, and the sprightly gremolata topping. All you need to go with it are haricot beans (3 cans should do it), heated with garlic and a little olive oil and roughly mashed, and some watercress.

Heat 2 tbsp oil in a large frying pan (or two pans, if you want to speed things up). Fry 2 oxtails, cut into 5cm/2in lengths, in batches until brown and slightly crusted on all sides. This takes a good 30 minutes (I usually read a magazine or get on with other kitchen jobs at the same time, since the meat needs the minimum of prodding and moving). Transfer the meat to a large casserole dish.

Add a little more oil if necessary, and cook 2 chopped onions in the same frying pan, until soft. Stir in 4 chopped cloves of garlic for the last minute or so. Scrape the whole lot into the casserole dish with the oxtail. Pour 500ml/18fl oz red wine into the frying pan and stir well as it bubbles up, scraping up the delicious gunk on the bottom of the pan, then tip into the casserole dish. Add 2 x 400g/13oz cans of tomatoes and 100g/4oz black pudding, peeled and chopped into pea-sized pieces, plus a fat pinch of salt.

Bring to simmering point, then reduce the heat to the minimum, cover and cook for about 4 hours, until the meat is soft and falling from the bone. (You can do this over 2 days if it's more convenient. Refrigerate for up to 3 days or freeze. Scrape off any fat on the surface and reheat.)

To make the gremolata, finely chop together the zest of 2 unwaxed oranges, 1 clove of garlic and a handful of basil leaves.

Adjust the seasoning of the stew and serve with a little orange and basil gremolata sprinkled over each helping. Serves 6–8.

*serves 4, when used for spaghetti bolognaise
  or cottage pie*

5–7oz/140–200g onions, peeled

5–7oz/140–200g carrots, peeled

1 stick of celery

2 tbsp olive oil

salt and pepper

1lb/450g mince

13oz/400g can of tomatoes, roughly chopped

7fl oz/200ml beef or vegetable stock
  (see pages188–9)

simple mince

CHOP THE VEGETABLES. Cut the onion, carrots and celery into little dice about
the size of a small pea.

FRY THEM SLOWLY in the oil over a low heat, with a generous pinch of salt (the
salt breaks down the cell walls of the onions, so that they soften and brown
more quickly). You want them soft and freckled with brown (about 20–30
minutes). Scrape the vegetables into a bowl.

BROWN THE MEAT. Raise the heat to medium and fry the meat in two batches,
each time spreading it out in a thin layer so that it covers the base of the pan in
a gappy way to let the steam escape, and not stirring for 10 minutes or so to get
a good mahogany brown. (A dull greyish beige just means that the meat has
steamed. It will have none of the vital flavours.)

SIMMER. Add the tomatoes, stock and cooked vegetables. Simmer very gently
for an hour or more until the mince is soft, not granular, spooning off any
excess fat which floats to the surface. If the mince is still too liquid at the end,
raise the heat and bubble until it's moist but not dripping with liquid.

SEASON. Taste the mixture and season it. Salt and pepper, of course, but a
splash of Worcestershire sauce, a dash of chilli sauce, or a pinch or two of sugar
are also worth considering.

good things to make with mince

A SOFTLY MELTING PILE of savoury mince is the base of countless recipes. It's the sort of crowd-pleasing food that is well worth doing, not least because people do it so little now. Make double quantities and freeze the extra and you'll be ready when hungry hordes descend.

CHILI CON CARNE

Just before adding the tomatoes to the mince, add 1 tsp ground cumin, 1 tsp paprika and a chopped red chilli (deseeded first if you want a milder chili) and stir for a minute. Then go ahead with adding the tomatoes, stock and vegetables. It's worth noting that the heat of fresh chillies varies enormously. Even those from the same bush can range widely, depending on whether they grew on the sunny or the shady side. Taste a scrap of each one to assess its power before adding it to any dish.

OTHER THINGS TO ADD TO CHILI

➤ A couple of grilled and peeled red peppers, roughly sliced, is a nice addition. Peeling the peppers is a bother, but worth it to avoid those tough ribbons of skin in the chili.

➤ Stir in a couple of cans of rinsed red kidney beans (somehow for a dish as kitsch as chili con carne, it doesn't seem right to cook them from scratch) to heat through at the end.

➤ Taste and add chilli sauce if it needs extra kick, and stir in a square or two of dark chocolate to add depth to the flavour.

➤ Serve liberally scattered with coriander leaves, with a fresh tomato salsa and sour cream mixed with chopped chives, plus rice or (even better) warm tortillas.

SPAGHETTI BOLOGNAISE

Serve the mince with spaghetti or (better) a flat pasta like papadelle or tagliatelle, and grated Parmesan cheese. The quantity given is enough for 4 people as a main course, served with 500g/1lb 2oz pasta.

SHEPHERD'S/COTTAGE PIE

Shepherd's pie (made with lamb mince) and cottage pie (made with beef mince) evoke a rural British idyll and feel like they must go way back. In fact the potatoes that are vital for the topping didn't become popular in the UK until the eighteenth century and the term 'shepherd's pie' isn't recorded until the 1870s. Not that it matters when either pie is so comfortingly delicious.

Top the mince with mounds of mashed potato, dot with butter and finish in a hot oven or under a grill, so that it is golden brown with dark crisp peaks. The same rules apply as for the potato on a fish pie (see pages 59 and 61 for instructions on consistency and for an alternative topping with sliced potatoes). Mince is more robustly flavoured than fish, so you can get away with fancier toppings than for fish pie. Try mashing swede or carrot, or both, with the potato, or flavouring it with rosemary-infused butter.

good things to add to a mince

❥ Cook a handful (about 55g/2oz) of black olives into the mince to give it a delicious richness. Don't bother with the ready-pitted ones, which are bland and rubbery. Choose pits-in olives instead, and stone them yourself, either with a sharp knife or a proper olive stoner – a useful gadget that can be used for cherries too. The best olives of all to use are the salty dry-cured ones. Add them at the same time as the tomatoes and remember that you'll need to add much less salt to the finished sauce. ➡

❥ A small sprig of robust herbs like thyme, oregano and bay can go in with the tomatoes. Liberal amounts of flat leaf parsley and basil are best stirred in just at the end.

❥ A couple of chopped anchovies fried with the vegetables make the mince more savoury and not at all fishy.

❥ Two chicken livers, chopped small and browned with the mince, make the mixture really meaty.

❥ A large aubergine cut into 2.5cm/1in cubes and fried with the onion until soft and golden.

❥ 500g/1lb 2oz fresh tomatoes (plum tomatoes are best). Peel them by plunging them into a pan of boiling water for 10 seconds, then drain and slip off the skins. Cut into quarters and scoop out the seeds with a spoon. Stir into the sauce just before serving and heat through so they are hot and just beginning to collapse.

❥ 200g/7oz smoked streaky bacon, chopped and cooked with the onion.

serves 2

1 pint/600ml well-flavoured chicken stock (see pages 188–9)

2oz/55g angels' hair pasta

2 chicken thighs, skinned and cut into grape-sized pieces

salt and pepper

a small bunch of dill, chopped

chicken noodle soup

HEAT THE STOCK AND ADD THE CHICKEN. Heat the stock to boiling point and drop in the pasta and the chicken.

SIMMER for 3–4 minutes, until the pasta and chicken are cooked.

TASTE AND SEASON. Taste and add salt and pepper if necessary, then ladle the soup into two bowls, scatter with dill and serve.

what you need to make noodle soup

FROM VIETNAM'S PHO to Japan's ramen, from Persian *ash-e reshteh* to European chicken noodle soup, pasta soups are loved by people the world over. And no wonder. A steaming broth, fragrant with spices or herbs and with little nuggets of meat and vegetables nestling amongst slippery noodles, is a warming, simple meal that can be ready in as little as 10 minutes.

THE STOCK

Homemade stock is the best starting point, and is easy to make (see pages 188–9), but it may not be to hand. Tubs of stock from the supermarket chill-cabinet will work fine, but they are expensive and lack that lip-smacking, gelatine-rich stickiness. For a beef noodle soup, tinned consommé makes a good store-cupboard late night supper.

THE NOODLES

Any noodles or long pasta will work, but if the spicing is oriental, Asian noodles will suit better than Italian, and vice versa. Don't forget the charming little Italian soup pastas like ditalini ('little thimbles') pastine or stelline ('little stars') or orzo (rice shaped pasta). Cook them in the hot stock, so that the pasta absorbs some of the flavour.

THE MEAT

This is fast food, so stick to tender cuts of red meat – steak and fillet. Cut the meat small, about the size of an olive, and it will cook in the same time as the pasta. Don't mince it, though. The pieces should be large enough to chew on, not like those strange little shreds of damp cardboard in tinned noodle soup.

With chicken, thigh meat has more heft and flavour than breast, which tends to go curiously dry. Very finely sliced raw meat (beef, pork, lamb, chicken or what you will) can be put in the serving bowl and the simmering stock and noodles poured over. It will cook in seconds in the heat of the stock.

Left-over cooked meat – the remains of the Sunday roast, for instance – can be used too, but cut it carefully into nuggets, removing any tough bits of gristle. Store them in the fridge, while you make a stock from the bones and squeeze every last drop of goodness into your soup.

THE FISH

Fish can be added, in cubes or slices, to cook briefly in the hot stock (use vegetable or fish stock – see page 189). Prawns are good, but if they are already cooked they should be heated through only briefly, or they will go tough and woolly. Bivalves such as mussels will release their own juices as they steam open, thus making their own stock base for a soup (see moules marinières, pages 68–9). Throw out any that don't open.

good flavourings for noodle soup

EUROPEAN-STYLE NOODLE SOUP

❯ Try a capful of brandy added to the stock and simmered for 5 minutes. It gives a roundness and a hint of acidity, even once the alcohol has boiled off.

❯ A strip of orange peel gives fragrance to a beef noodle soup, and however odd it may seem, a single star anise simmered in just about any meat stock will improve the soup.

❯ A small sprig of thyme (in chicken soup) or rosemary (in beef) are also good.

❯ Fresh herbs scattered over at the end make it feel more luxurious: dill is especially good in a chicken noodle soup.

GOOD VEGETABLES FOR NOODLE SOUP

Cut vegetables into small slices that will cook quickly and be easy to eat. I find root vegetables like carrots too sweet and texturally at odds with the meat and noodles, but here are some other ideas:

❯ Whole peeled cherry tomatoes are delicious and pretty in a beef noodle soup. Peeling them may seem like a faff, but it makes all the difference since the tough skins are at odds with the slippery-smooth noodles. To peel the tomatoes, just drop them in a bowl of boiling water for 10 seconds. Scoop them out, run under cold water, and split the skin with a sharp knife. It should then be easy to slip the skin off. If not, return the tomatoes to the boiling water for another few seconds.

❯ Young spinach leaves, added as you ladle the soup into bowls, so that they wilt but don't go slimy.

❯ Peeled broad beans in a chicken soup. To take off their grey-green coats, put in a pan of boiling water and cook for 30 seconds. Drain and rinse with cold water. Pierce the skin of each bean with your fingernail and slip out the bright green nugget within. It takes a few minutes, but it's absolutely worth it.

❯ Pak choi or bok choi, sliced and cooked for a minute, is lovely in Asian spiced soups.

ORIENTAL-STYLE SOUPS

The first three of the items listed below should be added early in the recipe, to have as long as possible to infuse the stock with their flavour:

❥ A bashed stalk of lemongrass, or a few kaffir lime leaves, add a delicious Asian citrus note to a simmering broth.

❥ If you find lemons or clementines with their foliage attached, these leaves – as long as they not dried out but shiny and flexible – work as well.

❥ Fresh ginger, either sliced or grated, is good.

❥ The fresh herbs that are so important in Oriental soups go into the soup at the end, be they mint, coriander, Thai 'holy' basil or a combination, and, for characteristic south-east Asian sourness, a good squeeze of fresh lime.

❥ Towards the end of cooking, a splosh of coconut milk is delicious, but rich. Think of it as double cream, so a quarter to a third of a 400ml/14fl oz pot is plenty for two people. Temper the creaminess with chilli and hand round those lime quarters to squeeze over.

good noodle soups to make

Beef pho ←

Pho, pronounced 'fer' as in 'offer', is Vietnam's take on noodle soup, and is sustaining and fragrant with fish sauce and lime. You need lots of herbs and vegetables to pile on at the table – a key part of the dish. While I'm not claiming that this recipe is especially authentic, it hits the same flavour notes as the original.

Heat 600ml/1 pint stock with a 2.5cm/1in chunk of fresh ginger (thickly sliced), 1 clove of garlic (chopped), 2 star anise and a good grind of black pepper. Simmer very gently for 30 minutes or so, topping up with water if necessary. Stir 1 tbsp fish sauce into the stock.

Add a bundle of vermicelli noodles (around 55g/2oz) and heat them through (about 30 seconds). Ladle into bowls and add a thinly sliced beef steak, which will cook in the heat of the stock. You could also use left-over roast beef.

To serve, scatter with a few coriander leaves and put more flavourings on the table for people to help themselves to: more coriander leaves, the leaves from a small bunch of mint, 4 spring onions (finely sliced), a handful of bean sprouts, a chilli (deseeded and finely sliced) and 4 lime wedges. Serves 2.

Duck noodle soup

Probably my favourite noodle soup of all, this one is inspired by a recipe in Sophie Grigson's *Meat Course*, a wonderful book now sadly out of print. I often buy a whole duck, then roast the breasts and casserole the legs. Very nice, but the best bit of all is this soup, made from the carcass.

Pour 1.5 litres/2½ pints duck stock into a pan, add a cinnamon stick and a star anise and boil down the stock until you have about 750ml/1½ pints of richly flavoured, fragrant broth.

Add 1 tsp soft brown sugar, 2 tbsp soy sauce, 1 mild red chilli (de-seeded and sliced) and 90g/3oz rice noodles. Simmer until the noodles are just done. Stir in any left-over scraps of duck you might have from roasting the bird, plus the sliced heart if that was used in the stock (it will still have a good flavour and texture) and heat through.

Ladle into bowls and sprinkle over 3 sliced spring onions and the leaves from a small bunch of coriander. Eat straight away. Serves 2–4.

serves 4–6

4 rashers of streaky bacon

2 leeks

a fist-sized chunk of green cabbage

1 large onion, peeled

2 sticks of celery

2 cloves of garlic

2 carrots, peeled

13oz/400g can of haricot or cannellini beans,
  drained and rinsed

13oz/400g can of tomatoes

3 pints/1.6 litres light pork, chicken or vegetable
  stock (see pages 188–9), or water

2oz/55g spaghetti, broken into short lengths, or
  small pasta such as ditalini (little thimbles)

salt and pepper

basil leaves and grated Parmesan cheese,
  to serve

minestrone

PREPARE THE INGREDIENTS. Cut the rind off the bacon and discard. Cut the
bacon into strips about the width of a pencil – scissors are easier than a knife
here. Slice the leeks (discard the tough, dark green bits) and cabbage. Chop the
onion, carrots and celery. Finely chop the garlic.

FRY THE ONION AND BACON in a large pan over a low heat until the
onion is softened. The bacon should provide enough fat, but add a little olive
oil if you like.

ADD THE REST OF THE VEGETABLES. Stir in the garlic and cook for another
minute, then add the rest of the vegetables, the beans, tomatoes (breaking them
up against the side of the pan with a wooden spoon) and stock or water.

SIMMER. Bring to the boil and simmer for about an hour.

COOK THE PASTA. Add the pasta and cook until soft (the time will vary
according to the type of pasta, but it should be softer than usual, not *al dente*).

STIR IN THE PARMESAN. Season with salt and pepper, and serve each bowlful
with a few ripped basil leaves, and more grated Parmesan.

how to make the perfect minestrone

FIRST A QUICK LESSON in minestrone-speak. *Minestra*, the root of the word minestrone, means soup, usually a medium-thick affair, while a *minestrina* is thin and more of a broth. A minestrone, then, is a big, thick, chunky soup. Too big for a first course, this is a one-pot meal of hearty peasant food.

The word *minestra* derives from the Latin *ministrare*, to serve, or to help. Although this probably stems from the Roman custom of having servants dish up the soup (other courses were put in the centre of the table for guests to help themselves), minestrone is a perfect way of ministering to our winter blues, soothing and restoring us. It's also one of the most agreeable ways I know of eating lots and lots of vegetables.

SLOW COOKING
The secret of a minestrone is long, slow cooking. To those of us used to cooking their vegetables lightly, this is counter-intuitive, but, trust me, it's the only way to get the rich flavour and unctuous texture.

IDEAL INGREDIENTS
In Italy, what's in a minestrone varies region by region. The only rules are that the vegetables should be local, seasonal and very fresh: don't even think of adding those sprouts that have been hanging around since Christmas! Some sort of starch is a must. Northern Italians add rice, southern Italians add pasta. Diced potatoes work too. I like to add tomatoes, even in winter, but they aren't compulsory. Nigella doesn't use them; Elizabeth David does.

CHOP CHOP!
Cut the vegetables with a reasonable amount of care: they need to be evenly sized to cook evenly, and neat shapes make a better-looking soup. Size is up to you, but somewhere between a pea and a grape is best.

good ways to eat minestrone

GOOD ADDITIONS
❥ Fresh pesto – stir a tablespoonful into each bowlful to make minestrone Genovese. ➡
❥ Half a small pumpkin or butternut squash, peeled and cut into small chunks, as they do in Lombardy.
❥ A chopped red chilli, one of the larger, mild ones.
❥ Aubergine or courgettes, diced.
❥ Swiss chard, the white stem sliced and the dark leaves cut into strips.

LEFT-OVERS
If anything, minestrone is even better the next day. Reheat it gently until it is just warm, not hot, and trickle with a little good olive oil. Or use left-overs to make a ribollita: put a thick slice of good bread (slightly stale, if possible) in each bowl and pour over the reheated minestrone. Add some steamed spinach or Savoy cabbage, if you like, and then drizzle with extra virgin olive oil.

FISH

serves 2

1lb/450g whole fish or 13oz/400g fish fillets
salt and pepper
4 tbsp olive oil

baked fish

PREHEAT THE OVEN to 190°C/375°F/Gas 5.

PREPARE THE FISH. Season the fish well with salt and pepper and trickle with oil (or dab with butter if you prefer). If using fillets, cover with foil to stop them drying out.

COOK THE FISH in the oven for 8–10 minutes per inch of thickness if baking whole fish. If using fillets, check after 6 minutes to see if they are done.

how to bake fish properly

TIME TO EAT FISH. Once we relied on fish as a cheap and delicious source of protein. Now we don't eat enough, and what we eat is the wrong kind: too much unsustainable cod and badly farmed salmon; too little omega-3-rich mackerel and herring.

Of course, much of it isn't cheap any more. But those mackerel and herring, along with sardines, and pollack and coley for white-fish lovers, are still bargains. When time is short – all too often in my household – fish takes minutes to prepare, making it perfect for the realities of working life.

TIMING

The exact timing depends on the fish – some fish have much tighter-grained flesh than others. And then, how to define perfectly done? Some fish, generally white fish like halibut or bass fillets, are best eaten when only barely cooked, still with a faint translucency about the middle of the fillet. Oily fish such as herring, sardines and mackerel, need to be cooked through or they are cloying.

So timings are never going to be exact. Start with 6 minutes, then test every few minutes to see if it is cooked.

FIRST ON THE HOB, THEN IN THE OVEN

Mitchell Tonks, fishmonger extraordinaire, recommends browning fish in a pan and then finishing the cooking in the oven. Although it's not the greenest way to cook fish (heating up the oven for so short a time), it does make for delicious crisp skin. It's not the best way for skinless fillet, however, as it could dry out.

Heat the oven as high as it will go, and on the hob heat a frying pan that can go in the oven. Pour a little oil into the pan and season the fish with salt, rubbing it well into the skin. Cook the fish skin-side down for about 4 minutes, or until the skin is golden and crisp. Turn with a fish slice and pop it into the oven for another 5 minutes for fillet or about 15–20 minutes for whole fish, until done.

HOW TO TELL IF FISH IS COOKED

Fish with skin: whole fish, and fillets cooked skin-side up, are the easiest to test. Press your finger gently on to the skin. If the fish is cooked, you should be able to feel the flakes of fish slipping apart beneath the skin. This method works for poached and fried fish too.

Fish fillets with no skin: the flesh will be opaque and quite firm, not bouncy, when touched. If you aren't sure, cut into a fillet with a small sharp knife, and bear in mind that the fish will cook on a little and 'set up' while it waits to go to the table.

good things to do with fish

Serve with a flavoured butter

Mix a handful of chopped parsley, dill or chives, or 1 tsp chopped rosemary, thyme or tarragon, into 55g/2oz soft butter. Add piquancy by beating in the juice of half a lemon or Seville orange, a small chopped chilli, or a can of anchovies, also chopped. Store the butter, well covered, in the fridge for up to a week (too long and the citrus juice will start to leak out), but don't use it while it is still chilly and hard. Instead, let it soften before dolloping it on to the fish (about 1 tbsp per person), so that it melts into the flesh.

Add a crust

Put a crust on a fillet: 4 tbsp fresh breadcrumbs mixed with freshly chopped herbs and lemon zest, plus 1 tbsp melted butter and seasoning. Spread evenly on to the fish fillets and bake as usual.

Roast fish with vine tomatoes and capers ➡

For a really crispy skin, bake whole fish at the highest temperature to which your oven will go.

Use whole fish, each about 225g/8oz (1 per person) or 450g/1lb (for 2), gutted and scaled. Bream and seabass work brilliantly, but so do chunks of salmon. You can use this recipe to cook a whole salmon, but make sure it's organic or from a reputable farm like Glenarm. Cheap farmed salmon is too oily for this.

Preheat the oven to 240°C/475°F/Gas 9, or as high as it will go. Boil 6 egg-sized new potatoes, cut into 1cm/½in slices, for 3 minutes until almost cooked.

Smear 1 tbsp olive oil over the base of a shallow roasting tin and put 2 small or 1 large fish, gutted and scaled, on top. Arrange the potatoes around, lay over 2 branches of cherry tomatoes, and scatter over 1 tbsp drained and rinsed capers. Drizzle over 3 more tbsp olive oil, smearing it over all the ingredients with your hands. Grind over salt and pepper.

Cover with foil and bake for 10 minutes, then remove the foil and cook for another 15 minutes, so that the potatoes brown nicely. Scatter with a few ripped basil leaves and serve. Serves 2.

serves 2

1lb/450g potatoes, peeled
¾ pint/425ml milk
4 tbsp butter
salt and pepper
12oz/350g fish fillets
1 tbsp plain flour

fish pie

PREHEAT THE OVEN to 180°C/350°F/Gas 4.

MAKE THE MASH. Cook the potatoes in well-salted water. Heat ¼ pint/150ml of the milk and mash the potatoes with 2 tbsp of the butter and the hot milk. The mash should be thick but light and fluffy. Season with salt and pepper.

COOK THE FISH. While the potatoes are boiling, pour the rest of the milk (½ pint/300ml) into a wide pan, and place the fish fillets, skin-side up, on top. Bring slowly to the boil, cover the pan and turn off the heat. Leave to stand for 5 minutes, or until any skin can be peeled off the fish and the flesh flakes easily.

MAKE THE SAUCE. In another pan, melt a a further 1 tbsp of the butter and stir in the flour. Cook for a minute, then stir in the milk from the fish pan. Cook, stirring, over a medium-low heat, until thick and smooth (put it through a sieve or blitz with a hand blender if it is obstinately lumpy).

ASSEMBLE THE PIE. Stir half the sauce gently into the fish, letting it fall in large flakes. Add the rest of the sauce gradually, stopping when you have a pleasant consistency. Scrape the mixture into an ovenproof dish. Top with the potato and dab the last of the butter on top. Bake for about 30 minutes, until browned.

what you need to make a good fish pie

A GOOD FISH PIE is a triumph of structural engineering, with texture all important. If the potato is too soft or there is too much sauce in the filling, the layers become mixed up and just like baby-food. Not soft enough, and it's a huge, soggy fishcake. But like all nursery food, a fish pie is simple and, given care and attention, one of the best dishes around.

THE FISH
This used to be easy: a nice bit of cod or some haddock maybe. Nowadays over-fishing has put both on the verge of extinction, making them somewhere between Dutch veal and giant pandas on the culinary no-no scale. Opt for bountiful (and cheap) pollack or coley instead, or possibly salmon, but avoid other oily fish, which will overpower the dish.

The only exceptions I make to my self-imposed cod embargo, are for organic farmed cod and fish caught in carefully managed waters such as those certified by the Marine Stewardship Council. Look for their blue label in fishmongers and supermarkets.

Sadly, it is mostly the supermarkets who are scrambling on board the sustainable bandwagon. Some fishmongers have been slower to catch on. I have come across fishmongers who say that their cod is fine because it comes from day boats or is line caught, and that overfishing is a myth and the seas are teeming with cod anyway. The first two points are moot, and as for the last two – well, they would say that, wouldn't they? But then, fishmongers are an endangered species themselves, and it's arguable that supporting them is as important as supporting ethical fishing.

THE SAUCE
The fish will need cooking first. If you put it in raw, it will make the sauce watery. Poach it in milk (add flavourings like peppercorns and bay leaves if you can) and then make a thick white sauce with the cooking liquor. Enrich it with cream, or even better crème fraîche, but keep it thickish, like a fruit yoghurt, or the potato will sink in.

THE TOPPING
Mash is the classic. Make sure it is light but not too soft and wet. Let the boiled potatoes dry in a sieve over the hot pan, then mash them while still hot into hot milk. Beat well to obliterate any lumps, or better still use a mouli-legumes, or vegetable mill – using electrical equipment like a food processor or blender is death to mashed potato, reducing it to a sticky, gloopy wallpaper paste. Alternatively make a rosti topping (see page 61).

good things to add to a fish pie

THE FISH LAYER

Something extra in the mix is a good idea, to add interest. Some recipes include scallops or monkfish, but buying expensive fish seems to miss the point of such a homespun dish, and anyway delicate flavours and textures are lost in the general *mélange*.

A handful of peeled prawns is a common addition, but like frozen peas they give a supermarket ready-meal quality to the whole affair. Hard-boiled eggs are traditional but risky: they tend to go rubbery when they're reheated in the sauce.

❥ The best bet is something smoky: use about one-third smoked white fish, or else a chopped-up rasher or two of grilled bacon.
❥ Some vegetables are another idea, making the fish go further and creating a one-pot meal. Try:

Sautéed leeks (2 medium)
Mushrooms, also sautéed (100g/4oz)
Chunks of steamed Jerusalem artichokes (200g/7oz)
Salsify, peeled, steamed and cut into chunks (200g/7oz)
Spinach, wilted in butter and squeezed dry (200g/7oz)

THE SAUCE LAYER

❥ Herbs (chives, chervil and tarragon, as well as parsley) liven things up no end.
❥ Add a dollop of English mustard.
❥ Stir a teaspoonful of curry paste into the melting butter.
❥ Replace half the milk with cocnut milk and infuse the sauce with a bashed lemongrass stalk as it simmers.

THE MASH

You can add things to the mash if you want to make the pie a bit more fancy. It has to be said that some colour differentiation between the top and bottom layers makes a more interesting pie. Try:

❧ 2 tbsp grain mustard.

❧ A chopped spring onion.

❧ 2 tbsp chopped chives.

❧ Grated cheese (about 30g/1oz – the amount depends on the strength of the cheese, so add it slowly, tasting as you go).

❧ A teacupful (225ml/8fl oz) of cooked mashed swede or carrot.

❧ A teacupful (225ml/8fl oz) of chopped blanched cabbage, colcannon style.

❧ A pinch of saffron strands infused in a couple of tablespoonfuls of hot milk.

If mash isn't your thing, light and crisp pastry, such as puff or filo, makes a good contrast, or you could do a Delia-style rosti topping (see the box below). A more restrained layer of sliced parboiled potatoes is delicious too. Arrange them in overlapping rows over the filling, brush them with butter and bake until well browned on top.

A ROSTI TOPPING

For two people, peel 450g/1lb potatoes and cut them into roughly egg-sized chunks. Cook in boiling salted water for 10 minutes, then drain and cool. Grate on a coarse grater and mix with 2 tbsp melted butter. Pile on top of the fish mixture, patting down just lightly, and bake as usual.

good fish pies to make

Saffron fish pie ◄

Saffron is the ultimate spice for fish, giving fragrance, rich flavour and golden colour. It is expensive, but just a pinch makes this pie a treat for two. This recipe is smart enough for a supper party, especially with the elegant sliced-potato topping and it is easy to double or quadruple the ingredients to feed more people.

Preheat the oven to 180°C/350°F/Gas 4. Cut 450g/1lb potatoes into pencil-thick slices and boil them in salted water for about 10 minutes, until almost, but not quite, cooked. Pour 300ml/½ pint milk into a wide pan and put in 225g/8oz fish fillets, skin-side up. Bring slowly to the boil, cover the pan and turn off the heat. Leave to stand for 5 minutes, or until any skin can be peeled off the fish and the flesh flakes easily. Put a pinch of saffron strands in 2 tbsp hot milk. In another pan, melt 1 tbsp of butter and stir in 2 tsp flour. Cook for a minute, then stir in the milk from the fish pan, and the infused saffron milk. Cook, stirring, until thick and smooth (put it through a sieve if necessary). Season, if needed, with salt and pepper.

Pull the fish apart into large flakes. Stir half the sauce and 2 tbsp chopped chives gently into the fish. Add the rest of the sauce gradually, stopping when you have the right consistency. Scrape the mixture into an ovenproof dish.

Top with the potato, arranging it in overlapping slices, and dab 2 tbsp butter on top. Bake for about 30 minutes, until browned. Serves 2.

Mackerel, bacon and mustard pie, with a parsley mash

Ask the fishmonger to fillet 3 large, spanking-fresh mackerel. Poach the fillets in milk until just done, then flake the fish, throwing away the skin and reserving the milk. Chop and fry 200g/7oz smoked streaky bacon until turning golden, then add 2 sliced leeks. Cook until the leeks are soft and mix with the fish and 1 tbsp grain mustard. Make a white sauce with the fishy milk, and carefully stir into the fish mixture along with the mustard and plenty of pepper. Top with mashed potato into which you have stirred the chopped leaves from a small bunch of parsley and a couple of sprigs of tarragon. Bake as usual. Serves 4–6.

serves 4

1½lb/675g cooked fish

1 egg

1lb/450g potatoes, peeled, boiled
  and mashed

salt and pepper

oil, for frying

for the coating:

about 4 tbsp flour, seasoned with salt
  and pepper

1 egg, beaten with 1 tbsp water and
  a pinch of salt

2oz/55g breadcrumbs

fishcakes

PREPARE THE INGREDIENTS. Remove any skin and bone from the fish. Beat the egg into the mashed potatoes and season with salt, and pepper too if you like.

MIX THE FISH AND POTATO GENTLY. Your hands are the best tool for mixing, since a spoon may break the fish up too much. The aim is too keep it in fairly large flakes.

FORM INTO CAKES. Put the mixture in the fridge to firm up if necessary before shaping it into patties with floured hands – I like mine a little smaller than a tennis ball, and flattened.

COAT WITH FLOUR, EGG AND BREADCRUMBS. Dip each fishcake in flour, then in beaten egg and then in breadcrumbs, making sure they are well coated.

FRY UNTIL GOLDEN. Heat a finger's depth of oil in a pan and fry the fishcakes gently until golden on each side.

how to make perfect fishcakes

FISHCAKES MAY BE the user-up-of-leftovers *par excellence,* but they deserve better. Cooked from scratch with fresh ingredients, they are enough of a treat for the smartest party, not just delicious but comforting too.

THE PROPORTIONS

Leaving aside those chewy Oriental fish patties, a traditional fishcake is a mix of fish and mashed potato. The mash gives soft texture and cohesion, but the fish is the star. Aim for a quarter to half of the fishcake as potato, but no more: too little fish looks mean.

THE MASH

Decent mash is key to good fishcakes. First off, choose the right potatoes, and don't rely on what's written on the bag: supermarkets have very strange ideas on what makes good mash. King Edwards are good and Estima and Desirée also work well.

Make sure that you drain the potatoes well after boiling, giving them a couple of minutes in the sieve over the hot pan and with a tea-towel over them to dry out properly. Then mash them while they are still hot with a masher, ricer or (best of all) a mouli-legumes – but never, ever use the food processor which turns any potato into gloopy stodge. Enrich the mash with plenty of butter rather than milk or it will be too soft.

THE CRISP COATING

Fishcakes can be fried with just a dusting of flour, but breadcrumbs and egg make the most delectably crisp outside. The breadcrumbs can be fresh or dried.

Fresh breadcrumbs are made most easily by removing the crusts from day-old bread and blitzing them in the food processor. They'll keep a day or so, but after that need storing in a bag in the freezer.

Dried breadcrumbs keep well, so make them on a day when you have been cooking something else in the oven and have a surplus of bread. Slice the bread thinly, remove the crusts and put them in the turned-off oven straight after taking out the other dish. Leave until pale gold and completely dry – the time this takes will depend on how moist the bread was. Grind the dried bread in the food processor, and shake through a sieve to get rid of lumps. Store in an airtight container for a month or more.

THE FISH

Most fish makes good fishcakes, but avoid over-fished types such as cod, unless it is from a sustainable fishery (for example, Marine Stewardship Council certified) or sustainably farmed. Poach the fish until it's just done, then skin, bone and flake into olive-sized pieces. Stir carefully into the mash, so as not to break it up too much.

THE EGG

Adding an egg to the mix isn't strictly essential, but it does give the fishcakes lightness. The extra moisture can make the mixture tricky to handle, though.

FRYING OR BAKING

Fry the fishcakes in a finger's depth of sunflower or other mild vegetable oil, until golden brown and hot through. Keep the heat at medium-high. Too hot and the fishcakes will burn before they are cooked. Drain them on a piece of kitchen paper and eat immediately.

Fishcakes can be oven-baked, but the breadcrumbs will need a little enrichment to help them brown to the right crispness. Either mix melted butter into the breadcrumbs – about 2 tbsp to a teacupful (55g/2oz) of breadcrumbs – before coating the fishcakes, or spritz the finished fishcakes generously with olive oil spray before putting them in the oven.

FREEZING FISHCAKES

Fishcakes freeze well. In fact, if the mixture is too moist to handle easily, get round the problem by shaping the cakes with two spoons, arranging them on a tray and freezing them. Once they are solid, take them out and go through the flour-egg-breadcrumb routine, working fast to dip them in the breadcrumbs before the egg freezes hard on the surface of the fishcakes.

Cook the fishcakes straight from frozen, frying until golden and then cooking through in the oven: about 20 minutes at 180°C/350°F/Gas 4 should do it.

good things to add to fishcakes

❧ **Tarragon:** Stir 1 tbsp chopped fresh tarragon into the mashed potato, then mix in 675g/1½lb poached salmon. One of the best fishcakes of all.

❧ **Parsley:** Finely chopped parsley, and lots of it, is good with all fish. The mix should turn a pale green flecked with dark green, so think in terms of 3 or 4 tbsp.

❧ **Other herbs:** 1 tbsp chopped lemon thyme is lovely with mackerel but strong herbs like rosemary and sage should be used only in tiny quantities. Basil and mint go black when chopped and mixed in, and should be avoided. However, pesto keeps its colour, so just stir it in. About 3 tbsp should do it, but taste the mixture and add more if you like.

❧ **Fragrant spices:** ½ tsp turmeric adds a pretty yellow colour and subtle flavour, while the seeds from 2 fat cardamom pods give scent as well as flavour.

❧ **Hot stuff:** Oily fish like mackerel needs extra bite, so add a dollop of horseradish or some grain mustard.

❧ **Lemon:** Add the grated zest of ½ lemon, either to the fishcakes – it is particularly good with oily fish – or to some mayonnaise to serve alongside.

ADDING THE BREADCRUMBS

The classic – and best – coating for a fishcake is a coating of flour followed by egg and then breadcrumbs.

Line up three dishes, one with 4 tbsp flour seasoned with a little salt and pepper, one with an egg beaten with 1 tbsp water and a pinch of salt (which breaks up the albumen and makes the egg more liquid), and one with about a teacupful of breadcrumbs (at least 55g/2oz).

Turn the fishcake in the flour, then in the egg, then in the breadcrumbs. I use one hand for the 'wet' work, and the other for the 'dry' and do this as a production line. Coated fishcakes will keep in the fridge for a few hours.

moules marinières

serves 2 as a starter,
   1 as a main course

1lb/450g mussels

1oz/30g butter

2 tbsp peeled and finely
   chopped shallots

4fl oz/100ml white wine

2–3 tbsp roughly
   chopped flat leaf
   parsley

PREPARE THE MUSSELS. Clean the mussels, rejecting broken or open ones.

COOK THE SHALLOTS. Melt the butter in a large pan (one with a lid) and cook the shallots until soft.

SIMMER THE WINE AND MUSSELS. Add the white wine and bubble up for a minute, then tip in the mussels. Cover and cook, shaking, over a medium-high heat, for 2–3 minutes. After this time check that the mussels are opening, giving them another minute or two if necessary.

SERVE UP. Taste the juices for seasoning – they probably won't need salt. Scoop the mussels into soup plates (chuck out any that haven't opened), and strain over the juices to get rid of any grit. Scatter with the parsley and serve straight away with crusty bread or chips.

how to make perfect moules marinières

MOULES MARINIÈRES is one of those great dishes that feels like a treat but costs very little money, time or effort. It is sexy, too, with all that sensual eating with one's fingers. Not for nothing is shellfish said to be an aphrodisiac.

Don't save mussels for grown-ups, though. Children love the fiddle and fuss and the prettiness of the shells, as well as the flavour of the sweet orange nuggets hiding within. Put a bowl in the middle of the table and they can get some target practice by chucking the shells in.

PREPARING THE MUSSELS

❥ Check each mussel and throw away any that:

1. Are not tightly closed, or don't shut when tapped firmly on the side of the sink.
2. Have cracks in the shell.
3. Are over-heavy for their size (which means they may be full of mud).

❥ Knock off any barnacles with a blunt knife.

❥ Scrub them clean in cold water, using a nylon scourer. All of this can be done earlier in the day.

❥ Just before cooking, pull off the straggly 'beards' (the byssal threads, which help the mussel cling to rocks) that hang out of the shell.

❥ After cooking throw away any mussels that don't open.

THE SAUCE

❥ Don't be mean with the butter: as well as cooking the shallots, it emulsifies with the wine and mussel juices to thicken the sauce. Straining the sauce is optional, but gets rid of the residue of grit which otherwise will collect at the bottom of the bowl.

❥ Choose a dry French or French-style white wine (a Muscadet is ideal), nothing heavily oaked.

❥ Onion will do at a pinch, although shallots have a finer flavour. Leeks are another thought. Lots of people add garlic, which is good too, but not vital.

❥ Parsley should be flat leaf and bouncily fresh – curly leaf parsley has too coarse a texture, unless it is very young.

SHELLFISH SAFETY

Shellfish poisoning is very unpleasant, but the small risk shouldn't put us off enjoying them, unless you are one of the unlucky people with a serious allergy.

As long as the mussels come from a reputable source and are alive when you cook them, there should be no problem eating them. Throw away any which are open before cooking, or closed after cooking, plus damaged ones, and you should be fine.

As for wild mussels gathered from the seashore, *caveat emptor*, or rather *caveat* eater. You must be confident that the waters that the mussels grew in were not polluted.

good things to do with moules marinières

❥ After removing the mussels from the cooking pan, quickly poach some cubes of white fish or salmon in the liquor, for an impromptu chunky fish soup. Eat with chilli-flavoured mayonnaise.

❥ Add 6 tbsp double cream or crème fraîche to the liquor and quickly boil down to reduce and thicken, then strain over the mussels.

❥ Add a sprig or two of tarragon or lemon thyme to the pan along with the wine, to give a gentle herb flavour.

❥ Add 1 tbsp grated fresh ginger, ½ tsp ground turmeric, a bashed stalk of lemongrass and a little sliced chilli with the shallots. Soften the shallots, add the wine and cook the mussels as usual, spooning them into soup plates. Add 140ml/5fl oz (about one-third of a can) of coconut milk to the liquor, bring to simmering point and pour over the mussels.

VEGETABLES

serves 2 as a main course, 4 as a starter

1 onion, peeled and finely chopped

2oz/55g butter

about 8oz/225g risotto rice

about 5fl oz/140ml dry white wine

1½ pints/900ml hot chicken stock (see pages 188–9)

4 tbsp grated Parmesan cheese

salt and pepper

risotto

COOK THE ONION in half of the butter in a wide pan until soft.

STIR IN THE RICE and cook for another couple of minutes, stirring all the time.

SPLASH IN THE WINE and keep stirring until it has more or less evaporated.

ADD THE STOCK A LADLEFUL AT A TIME, still stirring constantly. Wait until each ladleful has been absorbed and the mixture is no longer soupy, before adding the next. When the rice is cooked but still firm, stop adding the stock and stir in any additional ingredients.

STIR IN THE PARMESAN AND THE REST OF THE BUTTER. Taste and add salt and pepper. Serve straight away.

what you need to make a risotto

A GOOD RISOTTO, with firm but not hard rice suspended in a creamy, savoury sauce, is possibly the perfect comfort food. So how seriously should it be taken? Italophiles would have it made only with the freshest chicken stock and dedicated risotto rice, stirred incessantly and served instantly. More prosaic cooks insist that it's simply a moist rice dish, a good simple supper that's little trouble to put together.

The truth is that risotto is simple and quick and can be on the table in less than 30 minutes, but don't try to do anything else at the same time. A risotto needs tender loving care as well as the best ingredients if it's to be good eating, not just rice porridge. Keep it for kitchen supper with friends, and stir as you chat.

Once made, it's good on its own, followed by a simple leafy salad. But it's also magnificent as a side dish-cum-sauce: think of risotto milanese, a saffron risotto, with slow-cooked osso buco. A mound of silky risotto transforms a simple plate of grilled chops, too.

THE RICE
Risotto rice is easy to find nowadays, in a multitude of varieties.
❧ Arborio is the most widely available, and makes a good creamy risotto, but it quickly goes stodgy and doughy-tasting, so that the last mouthfuls aren't as good as the first.
❧ Vialone nano is less creamy, but clean-tasting. The grains are separate and quite soft, almost like pasta.
❧ Carnaroli is my favourite. It keeps a good texture and flavour, and is really creamy.

THE LIQUID
Best of all, by a long way, is homemade chicken stock (see page 188–9). It's not just that the flavour is better, it's the gelatine from the bones which give body and that delicious edge of stickiness. Tubs of stock from the supermarket chiller cabinet are okay, I suppose, although they don't have this gelatinous quality and are startlingly expensive. If it must be cubes, at least dilute them to half strength, or the risotto will taste of cube, not fresh ingredients.

Vegetable stock is the thing for vegetarian risottos, either homemade (see page 189) or made with bouillon powder such as Marigold. Fish and seafood risottos can be made with a light chicken stock or vegetable stock (see page 189). Fish stock, of course, is great provided it is mild. If it has been made with wine, there is no need to add extra when cooking the risotto.

A glassful of white wine or vermouth at the start of cooking adds a gentle acidity. Italian wine is the stuff to use. I like Prosecco in risotto, perhaps only because it's nice and frivolous to drink as one stirs.

THE PAN
There are special risotto pans available with wide bases that curve up, bowl-like, to the sides, making it easier to ensure all the rice is stirred. They are also of equal

thickness on the sides as on the base, so the heat carries evenly. Unless you make risotto every week, though, a good-quality wide pan, such as a sauté pan, will do well. It must have a capacity of at least twice the volume of the finished risotto so that stirring can be done efficiently.

how to cook a perfect risotto

THE ONION
When cooking the finely chopped onion (or shallot or leek) in butter, remember that risotto shouldn't be rich, but it's not fat-free either, so don't be mean: melt a good 2 tbsp butter for four people.

THE RICE
Stir in the rice only when the onion (or shallot or leek) is well softened. You need to cook for 2 minutes or so, until it turns opaque, like tiny beads of ivory, stirring all the time.

THE WINE
If you're adding wine, you need to let it bubble up and reduce to almost nothing.

THE STOCK
Only then can you add a ladleful of hot stock, before stirring until half reduced and then adding more, still stirring. You need to keep adding liquid and stirring until the risotto is almost done: this will take 18–20 minutes.

You may not need all the stock, or you may need more. Use hot water if the stock runs out, or indeed if the flavour of the stock gets too strong. Taste the mixture regularly, to judge the balance of flavour as well as the doneness of the rice.

Resist the temptation to pour in the stock all at once. Adding the liquid little by little, so that the rice grains bump and grind against each other as you stir, encourages the starch to form a creamy-textured sauce before the rice loses its bite. As Marcella Hazan, the first lady of Italian cooking, puts it pithily: 'Remember, risotto is not boiled rice.'

THE SPATULA
A heatproof silicone spatula is the best stirrer. Don't use a metal spoon, which can break the rice.

WHEN IT'S DONE
The perfect risotto is creamy, with rice that is firm but without a chalky centre. In Italy it's liquid enough so that you can feel the separate grains in your mouth and it can only just be eaten with a fork. Bear in mind that the risotto will go on cooking and absorbing liquid even on the plate, so take it off the heat when it's a little too liquid and slightly underdone.

There's a dodgy restaurant practice of finishing risottos with double cream, which makes them over-rich and sickly. Do as the Italians do: off the heat and stir in a final tablespoon or two of butter which adds gloss and a soft creaminess that they call *mantecato*. A handful of freshly grated Parmesan is traditional, except in fish and seafood risottos.

good risottos to make

Most risotto flavourings are added just before the end of cooking. Delicate leaves and herbs can be added fresh, as they wilt into the mixture, cooking in the residual heat. Other ingredients, such as asparagus or chunks of butternut squash, need to be cooked first and just heated through in the risotto. Theoretically, it should be possible to cook them in the pan with the rice, but the timing is just too hard to judge for most ingredients.

There are exceptions. Saffron and beetroot can be added after the wine, since both need time to bleed their gorgeous colour and flavour into the dish. Fresh mushrooms are sautéed with the onions, while soaked dried mushrooms can go in after the wine.

Above all, keep it simple and never use more than two additions. Too many ingredients in a risotto is reminiscent of cheap fried rice.

Early spring

❥ Sorrel leaves: add a handful or two raw (tough stems removed) a minute or two before the risotto's done; they'll cook in the heat of the dish.

❥ Wild garlic: a dozen chopped wild garlic leaves stirred in before the final butter (*mantecato*). Scatter garlic flowers over the finished dish.

Late spring and summer

❥ Asparagus or shelled peas: add 300g/10oz steamed trimmed asparagus or shelled peas. Scatter hot fried diced pancetta (about 55g/2oz) over the top.

❥ Broad beans: around 170g/6oz lightly cooked broad beans, peeled of their grey-green skins first (you'll need a good 1.2kg/2½lb beans in the pod). Add a pinch of saffron to the simmering stock for fragrance and colour.

❥ Clams: 300–450g/10oz–1lb clams, well washed and added when the risotto is almost done. Pop the lid on and shake until the shells steam open. Serve scattered with lots of chopped parsley.

Autumn and winter

❧ Beetroot risotto: 2 medium beetroot, finely grated, added with the first ladleful of stock for a glorious magenta risotto, good on its own with a dollop of soured cream, or with grilled lamb chops and some ripped chervil. Don't overdo the Parmesan, or the earthiness of the beetroot will be lost.

❧ Butternut squash: a small butternut squash, peeled, cubed and sautéed until soft, then stirred in at the end.

❧ Mussels: 225–450g/8oz–1lb mussels, added in the same way as clams (see page 75).

❧ Leek and scallops: scallops are particularly good in a risotto made with the sliced white part of 3 leeks. Choose hand-dived scallops in the shell if possible and avoid scallops that have been sitting in water, which will never brown properly. Pat 6–8 scallops dry (4 if they are huge) on kitchen paper and pierce the orange corals (if you have them) with a needle to stop them bursting when they cook. Cut the white part horizontally into two discs. When the risotto is nearly ready, fry the scallops for a minute or so on each side, just until golden, in a little olive oil. Serve on top of the risotto. ➡

❧ Mushrooms: 300g/10oz mushrooms, sliced and fried with the onion (saute the onion alone for 5 minutes first). Add dried porcini (15g/½oz will be enough) soaked in hot water for an especially good version. Add the soaking liquid (strain out the grit first) with the stock.

All year

❧ Fish: at least 200g/7oz (more if you are feeling generous) white fish or salmon, cut into skinless, boneless chunks. Add to the pan when the risotto is almost done and cover to steam for 3 minutes, or until the fish is just cooked. Lightly smoked fish is especially good.

❧ Saffron: add a fat pinch of strands with the first ladleful of stock. The deep yellow colour and fragrance will develop as you stir.

❧ Squid ink: a sachet of squid ink (buy it from a good fishmonger or deli) has an intriguing and delicious complexity, more Bovril-y than fishy. Just don't choose it for a first date, since it dyes your teeth an unappealing blue-grey.

❧ Lemon: grated lemon zest, used sparingly, is especially good in leek-based risottos.

serves 6

melted butter and finely grated
  Parmesan cheese for the ramekins

1 quantity of white sauce (see page
  178)

7oz/200g Gruyère cheese, grated

4 eggs, separated

salt and pepper

a pinch of freshly grated nutmeg
  (optional)

1 tsp hot English mustard (optional)

a cheese soufflé

PREHEAT THE OVEN to 220°C/425°F/Gas 7 and put in a baking sheet to heat
up. Brush the inside of six ramekins with melted butter and dust finely with
grated Parmesan cheese.

MIX THE BASE. Heat the white sauce, if cold, in a small pan. Take off the heat
and add the Gruyère cheese (or other flavouring). Stir until smooth, then mix in
the egg yolks.

TASTE AND SEASON. Add plenty of seasoning: salt and pepper and also mustard
and nutmeg, if you like. The mixture should be strongly flavoured.

FOLD IN THE WHISKED EGG WHITES. Beat the egg whites until stiff. Fold the
base mixture into the egg whites and scrape into the ramekins, filling them to
the top. Level off with a spatula, then use your thumb to wipe around the inside
edge of each ramekin to make a groove in the mixture.

BAKE AND EAT STRAIGHT AWAY. Put the soufflés on the baking sheet in the
oven and bake for 8–10 minutes until risen and golden. Serve immediately.

how to make a perfect soufflé

NO DISH HAS MORE MYSTIQUE than the soufflé.

People talk of soufflés in hushed, admiring tones and they are the pinnacle of show-off cooking. Appropriate then, that soufflé means 'puffed up' in French, since really it's just a lot of hot air. No need to get in a spin: a light-as-a-cloud concoction with crisp top, mousse-like inside and creamy centre is a breeze to pull off. Just remember to call the guests to the table before you take the soufflé out of the oven, or it may be sunk by the time they stroll in.

I am, of course, talking of hot soufflés here. Cold soufflés are really a sort of mousse, of which you can read more on pages 152–4.

THE BASE
To make a soufflé, start with the base. The simplest and most common is a white sauce. It can be made a couple of days in advance, but should be reheated in a pan before proceeding or it will be too stiff.

Flavour it with smoked fish, cheese (plus mustard or herbs), cooked and chopped spinach (squeeze it dry first), or a stiff vegetable purée (if it is a watery purée you'll need less milk in the sauce).

The consistency of the base matters. Too thick, and the weight will stop the soufflé rising, too thin and it will fall through the egg whites and make a layer at the bottom – great for those self-saucing 'magic' chocolate puddings, but no good if it's a fluffy soufflé you're after. Something like the consistency of Dijon mustard is about right.

Make sure the taste of the base packs a punch: all that air and egg white will dilute the flavours, so check that it tastes just a little over-seasoned before folding in the egg white. Add plenty of salt, pepper, smooth mustard and herbs if it needs them. It should taste just a little too strong.

THE EGG WHITES
Beating the egg whites to the right stage is very important. Think of the bubbles of egg-white foam as little balloons. They need to be fairly full of air, but not full-to-bursting. When the soufflé goes in the oven, and the air expands in the heat, there will be enough elasticity in the egg-white balloons for them to grow bigger (making the soufflé rise) rather than pop, causing the soufflé to sink.

You're looking for what cheffy types call a 'soft peak'. That's the stage when, if the whisk is lifted out of the bowl of froth and held upright, the egg white clinging to the whisk will start to stand up in a point, but the tip will curl to a little question mark. If it stands up straight, it's called a stiff peak and has gone a bit far.

THE DISH
Soufflés can be baked in just about any ovenproof bowl, even a gratin dish. But for the best rise, choose ones with straight sides, and aim to fill them seven-eighths full for the most impressive height. Use your thumb to wipe around

the inside edge of each dish to just below the level of the mixture before putting them in the oven: this makes for a messy thumb but a neat, evenly risen soufflé.

Soufflés can also be baked in one large dish, with a capacity of about 1.2 litres/2 pints for this quantity. The same rules apply: straight sides make the best rise. It will take about 25–30 minutes in the oven.

PREPARING THE DISH

Grease the inside of the dish or dishes heavily with butter. The easiest way to do this is to brush them with melted butter. Perfectionists can do as chefs do, and let the buttered dishes 'set' in the fridge, then brush on a second layer. It's important that the coating is thorough and even, so that the final 'gritty' layer sticks well.

This last, dry layer gives the mixture something to cling to, helping it rise. It adds to the flavour, too, making a delicious browned edge to the soufflé. For savoury soufflés, Parmesan has the most flavour, but if you think it would clash with the other ingredients use dried breadcrumbs. For sweet soufflés, use caster sugar.

Whichever you choose, put a tablespoonful into the just-buttered dish and tip around the base and sides until evenly coated. Tip away any remaining crumbs, Parmesan or sugar into the next dish and continue until they are all done.

A HOT BAKING SHEET

Put a baking sheet in to heat up with the oven. Baking the soufflés on the hot sheet will boost the rise.

NO PEEKING

For a good, even rise, the oven needs to have a well-fitting seal so that the temperature is constant. Don't open the oven door until the cooking time is up, or the sudden draught could turn your soufflé into a pancake.

SWEET SOUFFLÉS

Sweet soufflés can be made by replacing the white sauce with a well-flavoured fruit purée, or crème pâtissière flavoured with coffee, caramel or chocolate. Brush the dish with butter and dust with caster sugar rather than Parmesan. Fill it right up to the brim for a fruit soufflé – they rise particularly neatly. Bake at a somewhat lower temperature (190°C/375°F/Gas 5), since the high sugar content makes them prone to browning too much.

GOOD INGREDIENTS FOR SOUFFLÉS

➤ 250g/9oz cooked smoked fish, kippers especially, puréed and added to the white sauce.

➤ 350g/12oz Jerusalem artichokes, cooked and rubbed through a sieve. Stir into the white sauce and season the mix with 1–2 tbsp grated Parmesan cheese.

➤ 3 tbsp chopped herbs, or more to taste – try parsley, chervil and chives with a couple of tablespoonfuls of grated Parmesan cheese.

➤ 170g/6oz goat's cheese, stirred into the hot white sauce until it melts. Eat with a green salad dressed with a walnut vinaigrette and chopped walnuts.

good soufflés to make

Spinach soufflé ↤

Preheat the oven to 220°C/425°F/Gas 7 and put in a baking sheet to heat up. Brush the inside of six ramekins with melted butter and coat with grated Parmesan cheese.

Heat 1 quantity of white sauce (see page 178) until soft and mix in 225g/8oz chopped cooked spinach and 4 egg yolks. Taste the mixture and season with nutmeg, salt and pepper.

Beat 4 egg whites until stiff. Chop 6 anchovies into small pieces. Sprinkle a few chopped anchovies into the bottom of each ramekin. Fold the spinach mixture into the egg whites and scrape into the ramekins, filling them to the top. Level off with a spatula, then run your thumb around the very edge of each ramekin to make a groove in the mix.

Put the soufflés on the hot baking sheet in the oven and bake for 8–10 minutes until risen and golden. Serves 6.

Raspberry soufflé

Preheat the oven to 190°C/375°F/Gas 5. Put a baking sheet into the oven to heat up.

Purée 7oz/200g raspberries and rub them through a sieve. Mix into 225ml/8fl oz crème pâtissière, along with 1 tbsp crème de framboise (optional). Taste and add more caster sugar if necessary. Beat 4 large egg whites to soft peaks and fold into the purée.

Brush the inside of four ramekins with melted butter and dust liberally with caster sugar. Fill the dishes with the soufflé mixture right to the top, and level off with a spatula. Wipe your thumb around the inside rim of the ramekins, making a groove in the mixture.

Bake on the hot baking sheet for 9 minutes. Finish by dusting with icing sugar. Serves 4.

serves 4–6

butter

2lb/900g vegetables, thinly sliced or cut into
   small dice

salt and pepper

½–1 pint/300–600ml white sauce (see page
   178), or cream, or tomato sauce (see
   page 180)

for the topping:

1–3 tbsp breadcrumbs

1oz/30g cheese (optional)

a simple gratin

PREHEAT THE OVEN to 180°C/350°F/Gas 4 and generously butter a gratin dish.

LAY THE VEGETABLES IN THE DISH, seasoning between each layer. Pour over the sauce or cream.

PUT ON THE TOPPING. Scatter over the breadcrumbs and the cheese (if using), or dab the breadcrumbs with butter if you prefer.

COOK in the oven for 40 minutes, until golden and bubbling.

what you need to make a gratin

GRATINS ARE MY FAVOURITE sort of cooking. They're easy, can hang around for ages in a warm oven and are unbelievably moreish. The only hard-and-fast rules are that they should have a crisp top and the underneath should be meltingly soft or creamy (and ideally both).

THE VEGETABLES

Choose your vegetables, then cut them into cubes or thin slices. Anything that gives off a lot of water as it cooks, such as mushrooms or courgettes, will need sautéing on top of the stove first. Starchy vegetables are simpler, but if you mix them with tomatoes (which add a nice edge to a potato gratin) you'll need to precook those starch-rich vegetables or allow extra time in the oven, since the tomato acidity can harden them. Make sure you season the vegetables well.

THE FAT

Butter, not oil, gives the best flavour. Don't brown the vegetables, just cook off some of the moisture to avoid ending up with a soggy mess.

THE BREADCRUMBS

Just a few dabs of butter should be enough to ensure a browned and irresistible finish, except for a gratin based on tomato sauce, which will need breadcrumbs. Breadcrumbs are a good idea for many gratins, adding texture, but make it a fine layer. Their purpose is to soak up the butter or the oils from the cheese, not to add to the bulk of the dish.

THE CHEESE

Cheese should be well flavoured and used sparingly — aim for a vibrant scattering of just-crisping Gruyère or Parmesan, not a thick, rubbery layer of cheap Cheddar weeping oil.

THE DISH

You can use any shallow ovenproof dish, but make it one you're prepared to bring to the table, since the last crusty dark scrapings are just delicious — gratin is from the French *gratter* to scrape. Best of all, use an oval gratin dish: the shape helps the heat to spread evenly. White china is the classic, but cast-iron ones like Le Creuset's are useful since they can be used on top of the stove as well as in the oven. Just make sure the dish isn't too deep: 7.5cm/3in is plenty. The point of a gratin is that it should have a large surface area, to create lots of that crusty top.

how to make a perfect gratin

THE SAUCE

You've piled in your vegetables, now for something to moisten it. Stock gives the lightest result, white sauce is more rustic and filling, and tomato sauce gives flavour without undue richness. Cream is, of course, the most delicious.

This liquid gives the vegetables cohesiveness and makes a good contrast to the crisp topping. If there are breadcrumbs sprinkled over the top, this sauce must be thick enough that they don't get soggy. It must also be thin enough for the gratin not to be claggy, but have a pleasing looseness.

A white sauce, being flour-based, will withstand the heat well, and is a safe bet. Cream tends to split, or curdle slightly, in the high heat necessary to brown the top. In a potato gratin, the starch in the potatoes will minimize this, and anyway the pale colour disguises it. Sometimes I quite like the curds of cream in gratins such as the butternut squash gratin on page 88. With the slight starchiness of squash, more starch, in the shape of flour in the sauce, seems unnecessary.

If cream or white sauce seems too rich, opt for tomato sauce (see page 180), which works well with Mediterranean vegetables such as courgettes. Cook it well first, especially if it is made with canned tomatoes, so that it has a mellow rather than acidic flavour, and top the dish with breadcrumbs dotted with butter, since it won't brown otherwise.

THE COOKING

Some people grill their gratins quickly, but unless it's a delicate affair made with hollandaise, I'm against that. A long stint in the oven is the thing, to get the proper melding of flavours and that divinely caramelized base. Butter the dish well to achieve this – at least a tablespoonful of soft butter smeared around the base and sides.

good seasonal gratins

For all of these, use 900g/2lb of vegetables, and bake for 40 minutes as in the main recipe (except for asparagus).

Winter

❥ Jerusalem artichoke gratin: Peel and slice the artichokes and bake with 300ml/½ pint double cream and a little garlic.

❥ Bacon gratin: Boil sliced potatoes for 10 minutes, drain and mix with 4 rashers of bacon, chopped. Bake with 300ml/½ pint white sauce (see page 178; let it down with milk to double-cream consistency) and top with grated Gruyère cheese.

Spring

❥ Spinach gratin: Wash 900g/2lb robust spinach leaves (not baby salad leaves, which turn to mush when cooked), drain and remove the tougher stems. Put in a hot pan, cover and cook in just the water clinging to the leaves for 3 minutes until wilted. Drain and tip the leaves into a bowl of iced water. When cold, drain and squeeze dry in a tea-towel. Mix in 2 tbsp melted butter, 2 tbsp double cream, salt, pepper and grated nutmeg. Spread out in a gratin dish (no more than 3cm/1in deep) and top with 3 tbsp double cream and 4 tbsp grated Gruyère cheese. Bake for 20 minutes until hot through, golden and bubbling. Serves 3–4

❥ Asparagus: special and expensive, asparagus deserves special treatment. Steam a bunch until just done, then tip into ice-cold water to cool. When you are ready to eat, lay the asparagus in a single layer in a heatproof dish. Scatter with a mixture of 3 tbsp fresh white breadcrumbs, 2 tbsp grated Parmesan cheese and 1 tbsp chopped herbs – parsley and chervil are best. Drizzle with 2 tbsp melted butter and cook under a hot grill until just done.

Summer

❥ Courgette gratin: Use half and half tomatoes and courgettes. The tomatoes should be skinned, deseeded and cut into quarters and the courgettes should be sliced into ½cm/1in slices. Sauté with a little garlic in a wide pan until dryish, then bake in a gratin dish with a scattering of breadcrumbs on top.

Autumn

❥ Mushroom and potato gratin: sauté 140g/5oz sliced mushrooms until soft, adding a fat clove of crushed garlic for the last 5 minutes. Simmer 900g/2lb sliced potatoes and a bay leaf with 300ml/½ pint double cream and 300ml/½ pint milk for 10 minutes, then add the mushrooms. Spread in a buttered gratin dish and bake.

❥ Pasta, leek and bacon gratin: mix one quantity of white sauce (see page 178) with 300ml/½ pint milk to make a double-cream consistency. Stir in 200ml/7fl oz crème fraîche, 4 fat leeks (sliced and sautéed), 225g/8oz bacon (chopped and sautéed) and 1 tbsp grain mustard. Scatter with grated Parmesan cheese and bake as usual.

good gratins
to make

Dauphinoise potatoes

The most famous gratin of all, and worth knowing off by heart, since producing a good Dauphinoise off the cuff is the best way I know of making friends and influencing people. Cooking the potatoes on top of the stove first speeds up the cooking time and also denatures the protein in the milk and cream, making the dish less likely to split.

Preheat the oven to 150°C/300°F/Gas 2. Peel 450g/1lb potatoes and cut into 3mm/⅛in slices. Don't wash the potatoes as the potato starch helps make the gratin creamy. Finely chop 1 clove of garlic and mix with the potatoes. Put them into a saucepan with 300ml/½ pint milk. Season generously with salt, pepper, cayenne and nutmeg. Bring to the boil and cook for 4–5 minutes. Take 140ml/5fl oz double cream and pour half into the potatoes and bring to the boil again. Remove from the heat and taste to check the seasoning, then mix in the rest of the cream. Pour into a buttered gratin dish in a layer no more than 2.5cm/1in deep. Dot with butter and bake for 1½ hours. Serves 4 (or 2 greedy people).

Butternut squash and shitake mushroom gratin ➤

Preheat the oven to 180°C/350°F/Gas 4. Melt 2 tbsp butter in a pan, add 100g/4oz shitake mushrooms, quartered, and cook just until they soften. Stir in 2 chopped sage leaves and 450g/1lb butternut squash, peeled, deseeded and cut into 2cm/¾in cubes, turning them in the mixture until coated. Use another tablespoonful of butter to grease a gratin dish, then tip the vegetables in and spread them out: they should be no more that two pieces deep, and loosely packed. Season generously with sea salt and lots of freshly ground black pepper, then drizzle over 6 tbsp whipping cream. Scatter over 30g/1oz grated cheese – Gruyère, Parmesan or Cheddar – and sprinkle with 2 tbsp breadcrumbs. Bake for an hour, until well browned. Serves 2–4.

GOOD THINGS TO ADD TO GRATINS

➤ Herbs or spices, or 3 or 4 rashers of bacon, chopped, are good additions but don't overcomplicate things: the main ingredient should be the star.
➤ Sautéed onions are delicious, but limit to a couple of tablespoonfuls. Too many too well-caramelised onions can make a potato gratin cloyingly, weirdly sweet.
➤ Grated lemon zest is lovely in the breadcrumb topping, especially right for spring gratins.

serves 2

2–3 tbsp olive oil
2lb/900g vegetables
salt and pepper

roasted vegetables

PREHEAT THE OVEN to anywhere from 180ºC/350ºF/Gas 4 to 230ºC/450ºF/Gas 8, bearing in mind that the higher the temperature, the shorter the time the vegetables will take to cook. Pour the olive oil into a roasting tin and put in the oven.

PREPARE THE VEGETABLES. Cut your vegetables into roughly even-sized chunks: matchbox-size or thereabouts.

CHUCK THE VEG IN THE TIN AND SEASON WELL. The vegetables should fit in a loose, not tightly packed, single layer. Toss them in the oil, using two spoons, and season with salt and pepper (and herbs or spices, if you like).

ROAST UNTIL BROWNED AND SOFT. Slap the vegetables in the oven and cook for 30 minutes to 1 hour, depending on the oven temperature.

what you need to roast vegetables

DO ROAST

❧ Root vegetables: beetroot, parsnips, carrots, salsify, sweet potatoes and yams. In moderation: Jerusalem artichokes, celeriac, turnips and swede – they have strong flavours which can overpower the mix.

❧ Onions, shallots, fennel and chicory: cut them into wedges through the root end so that they stay in chunks.

❧ Asparagus: as long as it is at least a finger thick. Works really well with grated or shaved Parmesan cheese.

❧ Red and yellow peppers: but not green or purple (which are just green under the skin) as they go bitter.

❧ Pumpkin and butternut squash: peel and deseed first, or leave the skin on and cut into wedges for a quicker fix.

❧ Aubergine: no need to salt them first for modern varieties, but be careful on holiday abroad – those pretty aubergines in the market may be too bitter for this treatment.

❧ Tomatoes: roast on their own since their juices will inhibit the other vegetables from browning. Cherry vine tomatoes look prettiest left whole on the stem. Cook them on baking parchment so that they don't burst as you lift them off. Large tomatoes should be halved through their equator and laid cut-side up on a baking sheet. Roast just until the skin is shrinking down a little and the top is darkening slightly. They will shrink to wrinkled, intensely flavoured jewels as they cool. Add them to couscous salads or eat with lamb.

❧ Garlic: roast in the skin for sweet intensity, then squidge on to fat slices of toast.

THE OIL

Olive oil is the standard, since sunflower and vegetable oils are too bland. Nut oils, especially walnut, are worth experimenting with for root vegetables, although the flavour may be too strong. Bacon fat is delicious, as are the drippings from a roast.

DON'T ROAST

❧ Salad vegetables (except tomatoes and chicory).

❧ Courgettes: the outside darkens but the inside turns to watery mush.

❧ Broccoli: generally toughens unappealingly, although young florets can sometimes be coaxed to an interesting caramel.

❧ Peas and beans.

❧ Sweetcorn: although this is excellent cooked until lightly charred under the grill or on the barbecue.

how to make perfect roast vegetables

STICKY, WITH DARK BROWN EDGES, soft yet chewy and toffee-sweet: roasting is the ideal way to brighten up winter root vegetables and to get the best from summer Mediterranean vegetables. The success of the method relies on two factors. You need to allow some of the moisture to be cooked off, so the flavours at once soften and intensify, and you need to get the natural sugars in the vegetables to caramelize to that delectable savoury-sweet crust.

PREPARATION
Scrub the vegetables first, then peel them if you want to: it's not vital, except for celeriac which is impossible to get completely clean. Peeled root vegetables will caramelise better on the outside, and so be more delicious.

THE SIZE
Cut the vegetables into chunks. We're aiming for a good balance of that caramelized outside and soft, sweet, steamed-in-its-own-juices inside. Too small, and the pieces will be hard. Too large, and there won't be enough of the delicious outer layer. The ideal size? Around the size of a matchbox or a fun-sized Mars Bar.

THE OIL
Vegetables, with their lower starch content, won't ever develop that crunchy surface that roast potatoes do. So there is no reason to use so much fat in the roasting tin as one would with potatoes. Indeed, the finger depth of fat that's so fantastic for roast potatoes would make other vegetables greasy. You just need enough oil to coat the vegetables.

good roasted vegetable dishes

Roasted chicory

Pale, satiny torpedoes of chicory tend to be eaten as a salad, but they are even more delicious roasted to a dark-edged caramel. Blanching them first rids them of excessive bitterness and leaves just a little edge to balance the sweetness. I'd happily eat these on their own with just some bread to wipe around the roasting tin, or they are excellent with roast beef.

Preheat the oven to 190°C/375°F/Gas 5 – or whatever temperature you are cooking the meat at.

Bring a pan of water to the boil. Halve 8 whole chicory lengthways, pulling off any damaged outer leaves. Drop the chicory in the water and boil for 2 minutes. Drain and run under the cold tap, then squeeze dry in a tea-towel. Arrange the chicory, cut-side up and tightly packed, in a small well-buttered roasting dish. Smear liberally with more butter and sprinkle with salt. Bake for about 30 minutes, until well browned and wilted. Serves 4.

GOOD THINGS TO DO WITH ROAST VEGETABLES

❥ Hot from the oven, roast vegetables go with all kinds of cooked meat.
❥ Delia made famous the roast Mediterranean vegetable/goat's cheese/harissa/couscous combination. It's just as good with root vegetables and a little crumbled feta cheese.
❥ Tumble the vegetables on to a bed of rocket or watercress and dress with a honey, balsamic vinegar and olive oil dressing.

Roasted fennel with Parmesan

Preheat the oven to 200°C/400°F/Gas 6. Cut 2 large heads of fennel through the root end into 2cm/¾in wedges. Pour 3–4 tbsp olive oil into a roasting tin and turn the fennel wedges in it. Arrange them neatly on their sides, season with salt and pepper and scatter over 4 tbsp grated Parmesan cheese. Roast for about 30 minutes. Serves 4.

Salad of roasted aubergine and tomatoes with feta and mint ➥

Preheat the oven to 200°C/400°F/Gas 6. Slice a large aubergine in half lengthways and then across into half moons about 1cm/½in thick. Toss in 2 tbsp olive oil mixed with a crushed clove of garlic and spread out on a baking sheet.

Slice 7 medium tomatoes (plum tomatoes are best) in half and lay, cut-side up, on another baking sheet. Drizzle with olive oil and sprinkle with salt.

Roast the aubergine on the shelf above the tomatoes for about 30 minutes until soft and browned, and roast the tomatoes until they are wrinkled (they will collapse more as they cool). Keep an eye on the tomatoes, as they may need to come out a few minutes earlier than the aubergine.

Toss the vegetables together and leave to cool to room temperature. Scatter over 30g/1oz crumbled Greek feta (it doesn't sound much, but the flavour is powerful) and the leaves from a small bunch of mint. Season with salt and pepper and drizzle with a little more olive oil. Serves 4 as a starter or side dish, or as part of a mezze.

GOOD THINGS TO ADD TO ROAST VEGETABLES

❥ A trickle of honey speeds the browning and adds mellow sweetness.
❥ 2 tsp cumin seeds.
❥ Just a smidge of curry paste with root vegetables, especially parsnips, mixed in with the oil.
❥ Chopped garlic, but added towards the end of cooking as it burns easily.
❥ Fine semolina – tossing the root vegetables in a couple of tablespoonfuls of semolina before turning in oil makes them crisper.

serves 4

8oz/225g potatoes per person
oil or lard
salt and pepper

roast potatoes

PREHEAT THE OVEN to 190°C/375°F/Gas 5.

PREPARE THE SPUDS. Peel the potatoes and cut into pieces no smaller than half an egg.

BOIL THEM. Put the potatoes into boiling, salted water and cook them for 10 minutes exactly.

DRY THE SPUDS AND ROUGH 'EM UP. Drain the potatoes in a colander, cover with a tea-towel and leave to dry for 5 minutes or so. Give the colander a good shake to rough up the surfaces.

GET THE FAT FIERCELY HOT. Heat the fat in a roasting tin in the oven. It needs to be at about little-finger deep. Put the roasting tin on the hob and heat until the fat is actually bubbly.

ADD THE SPUDS – CAREFULLY. Spoon the potatoes in at arm's length: they'll splash and spit.

ROAST FOR AROUND 30 MINUTES. Turn the potatoes in the fat and place in the oven (top shelf) for 15 minutes. Turn again, then roast for another 10–15 minutes, until well bronzed.

SERVE STRAIGHT AWAY. Scoop the potatoes into a serving dish, scatter with salt and eat immediately.

what you need to make roast potatoes

MASH MIGHT BE GREAT for a Saturday casserole, baked potatoes are fine for supper, but only roast potatoes will cut it for Sunday lunch. Getting them right revolves around timing. While the meat can – in fact, should – hang around for a bit or 'rest' before eating, the roasties need to come out of the oven after everyone's already sitting down at the table, to be at their crispest, fluffiest, steamiest best.

THE TIN

The roasting tin must be big enough for the potatoes to sit in a single layer, well spaced. If they are too close, the trapped steam will stop them browning properly. A decent-quality tin is safest since it won't warp in the high temperatures and can be put on the hob without problems. Mermaid is a good brand.

THE FAT

For a couple of years, goose-fat roast potatoes have been gourmet's choice, but there are other options. Here's how they cook up.

Lard: nice and crisp, with a hint of bacon flavour, slightly fatty. Great with lamb or pork.

Dripping: gloriously crunchy with a deeply savoury, Bovril-y taste. The *sine qua non* of a roast-beef dinner.

Sunflower oil: crisp, and with a picture-perfect even colour, but a distinctly chip-shop flavour. To be avoided.

Duck fat: less crisp, and with a pleasingly patchy colour, but with a deliciously savoury flavour that's perfect with roast chicken.

Goose fat: expensive but gives a to-die-for, biscuity-crisp outside, delicately savoury inside. Top choice for Christmas dinner. It's available in cans from Waitrose or Sainsburys and delis.

Olive oil: slow to reach a perfect brown and with a bland flavour.

Olive oil and a dollop of butter: it sounds counter-intuitive, since butter would burn at the high temperatures necessary for roasting, but some butter in the oil helps the potatoes colour up and gives a good caramel flavour. It's the best option if there are vegetarians coming to lunch.

THE OVEN

The steam created by the roast will inhibit proper browning of the potatoes, so best to finish them after the meat has come out of the oven and is resting.

THE POTATOES

There are all-round potatoes, which will cover most eventualities. Desirée is my default variety. For a special meal, though (and roast potatoes make it a special meal), it's worth picking up the right kind. Here's a round-up of what you can expect from some commonly available potato types.

❧ Estima: bland and dense.

❧ Desirée: very dry, which makes them perfect for mash but a bit mealy for perfect roasties.

❧ Marfona: too waxy for roasting.

❧ King Edward: properly fluffy, mild flavour.

❧ Maris Piper: moist and deliciously nutty, these are the top choice for roasting, although they don't make good mash.

good things to add to roast potatoes

SHALLOTS
Halve and peel 8 small shallots, or quarter 4 of the larger, copper-coloured banana shallots, and add them to the roasting tin. Shallots have a richer flavour when roasted than onions, which can be over-sweet and bland. They are also a neat size, and hold their shape well. Toss in a couple of sprigs of sage if you like.

ROSEMARY
Put a couple of sprigs in the roasting tin and chop the leaves from another couple of sprigs to scatter over 5 minutes before the end of the cooking time.

THYME
Tuck the sprigs from half a large bunch in with the potatoes, then scatter the leaves from the rest of the bunch over just before the end of roasting.

GARLIC
Chop a couple of cloves and scatter over 5 minutes before the end of the cooking time. Good in combination with rosemary.

SEMOLINA
Toss the potatoes in fine semolina just before tipping them into the hot fat, for the crunchiest potatoes of all.

serves 4

2 fat leeks, sliced

2oz/55g butter

salt and pepper

2 medium floury potatoes, peeled and cut into small cubes

1½ pints/900ml pints water or stock (see pages 188–9)

a little cream or chopped herbs, to serve

soup

COOK THE LEEKS SLOWLY IN THE BUTTER until soft, but without letting them colour. Season lightly with salt and pepper.

ADD THE POTATOES. Stir in the potatoes until well coated in butter and cook for a minute or two longer.

ADD THE WATER AND SIMMER. Pour in the water (or use a light stock if you prefer) and simmer for 20 minutes or so, until the potatoes are soft.

PURÉE THE SOUP. Liquidize or pass through a mouli-legumes. Taste and check the seasoning. Reheat and add a little cream or chopped herbs before serving.

BEST SOUP GADGETS

Even with chunky soups, it's likely that part of the mix will need to be blended to give the soup body. Use a liquidizer or blender, and for real perfection pass it through a fine sieve afterwards. A stick blender in the pan won't achieve quite such smoothness, but it is a convenient gadget and perfect for everyday soups. Food processors chop, not blend, so they won't give the proper smoothness.

When it comes to liquidizing soups, there are plenty of flashy gadgets around. Surprisingly, though, the best soups are often those put through a low-tech food-mill, the hand-cranked machine called a mouli-legumes. These power-sieves get rid of coarse bits in the way a blender can't, but retain just a hint of nubbly texture. It'll also make the lightest, creamiest mashed potatoes ever. A stainless-steel one is the kind to go for, so that the bits can go in the dishwasher.

how to make a good soup

SUBSTANTIAL SOUPS make fantastic meals. Dress them up with croûtons, creams or oils and have some good bread and cheese alongside. A leek and potato soup, such as the one opposite, is thrifty and delicious, and it's also easy to adapt. Just add a generous amount of whichever vegetables are to hand, cooking them at the same time as, or instead of, the potatoes.

LEEKS

These are a better bet than onions for the base. They give a gentler flavour.

SWEATING THE VEGETABLES

Don't try to save time by throwing all the vegetables in the pan with the water and boiling them. The sweating of the vegetables draws out their natural sweetness and intensifies their flavours.

The time to add any vegetable which needs cooking – carrots, say – is once the leeks are really soft. They shouldn't go brown, just lose all trace of crunch or raw flavour. Then stir in the potatoes and other vegetables.

Leafy vegetables, such as spinach, sorrel and watercress, should be added at the last minute or they will lose their vivid colour. Simmer the stems first to soften, then add the leaves and liquidize immediately.

WITH OR WITHOUT POTATO

If the vegetable is a starchy one – sweet potato, say – or if it is a light soup you're after, one to start a meal rather than a main course, consider dispensing with potato; though a small amount of spud does give a particular mouth-coating quality that is very satisfying.

For tomato soup, use only small amounts of potato, if any, or the soup will be too pale. Let it cook well in the butter before adding the tomato, which has acids that might otherwise harden it. Or follow the method for tomato sauce (see page 180) and let it down with extra stock to make a soup. Finish with a glug of cream.

STOCK

A good stock is a great foundation for a soup, but it must be restrained so that the finished bowlful tastes of the main ingredient, not of meat bones. A soup like the one opposite is actually just as good made with water. Cubes should always be made half strength or there'll be a whiff of foil wrappers about your carefully made potage. Milk is good in potato soups, giving a soft sweetness to the mix.

ENRICHMENT

A dollop of cream stirred in at the end makes the soup luxurious without adding too much richness. An alternative, especially good in watercress soup, is to add an egg yolk beaten with a ladleful of hot soup, from the pan. Stir over a gentle heat, as if you were making a custard, until it thickens slightly.

good things to add
to soup

OILS
❧ Trickle single-estate olive oil over rustic soups.
❧ Make a vivid green oil to spoon over potato or bean-thickened soups by puréeing basil, coriander, mint or parsley with olive oil, salt and a scrap of garlic.
❧ Fragrant truffle oil works on leek or mushroom soup.
CROÛTONS
❧ Cut light-textured bread into little cubes, and toss in olive oil with grated Parmesan cheese, chopped thyme, cumin or cayenne. Bake for 5–10 minutes at 190°C/375°F/Gas 5.
❧ For more rustic breads like ciabatta, slice day-old bread very thin, and trickle with olive oil, then bake as above to make crisp wafer-croûtons.
CREAM
❧ Whipped cream gives an ethereal lightness to soups, moussing on the surface.
❧ Soured cream has a lemony tang; mellow crème fraîche is richer.
❧ Mix lemon zest, chopped herbs or horseradish – quantities according to taste – into thick cream, crème fraîche or Greek yoghurt and pass around for dolloping.

good soups to make

Beetroot and cardamom ➡
Cook the leeks as on page 100, and stir in the crushed seeds from 2–3 fat cardamom pods. Cook for a minute, then add about 350g/12oz peeled and cubed beetroot instead of the potato and continue as for the basic recipe. Ready-cooked beetroot can be used and makes for a really fast soup, but make sure that it's the kind cooked without vinegar. That said, a squeeze of lemon juice at the end will improve the flavour.

Sweet potato soup with Angostura bitters
Sounds unlikely but it's a magic flavour combination. Use about 350g/12oz sweet potato instead of the regular potato and finish the soup with a few drops of Angostura bitters.

Mushroom and thyme
Cook 450g/1lb sliced mushrooms and a good sprig of thyme with the leeks. Add the potatoes and continue as for the basic recipe. Fish out the thyme before liquidizing.

Butternut squash and harissa
Cook the leeks, then stir in ½ tsp of harissa (see page 21). Cook for a minute, then add 1 large butternut squash, deseeded peeled and cubed, instead of the potato. Taste the finished soup and add more harissa if you like.

FLOUR & EGGS

serves 4

oil, for frying

2 leeks or onions, sliced

1½lb/675g casseroling meat, cubed

2 tbsp flour, seasoned with salt and pepper

1 pint/600ml stock (see pages 188–9)

8oz/225g puff or shortcrust pastry (see page 124)

1 egg, beaten

a savoury pie

FRY THE ONIONS AND MEAT. Heat 1 tbsp oil in a large frying pan and add the leeks or onions. Fry until golden, then scoop out and keep to one side. Toss the meat in the seasoned flour. Heat another 1 tbsp oil in the pan and brown the meat in batches, adding more oil if necessary.

DEGLAZE THE PAN. Tip half a teacupful (around 4fl oz/100ml) of stock into the empty pan and bring to the boil, stirring and scraping up all the gunk. Add the rest of the stock and whisk until smooth.

SIMMER THE MEAT. Tip the meat and this sauce into a flameproof casserole dish and simmer gently for 1–1½ hours, until the meat is tender. Allow to cool.

COVER WITH PASTRY AND BAKE. Preheat the oven to 200°C/400°F/Gas 6. Tip the mixture into a pie dish just large enough to take it all (around 2¼ pints/1.3 litres). Roll out the pastry a little larger than the top of the dish and cover the meat (see opposite). Brush the pastry with the beaten egg and slash it in a couple of places to make a steam vent. Bake for about 30 minutes, until golden and steaming hot.

how to make a perfect pie

PIES ARE ABOUT DRAMA. Plunge the knife into the shiny, gold top crust to let loose a rush of savoury, hunger-inducing steam and everyone's attention is grabbed. But what makes a really good pie? Two things are key: a well-flavoured filling and good pastry.

UPPER CRUST AND DOUBLE CRUST

Homemade meat pies tend to be top-crust only and this is the method I've given for the basic recipe. If you do want to opt for a double crust, use shortcrust rather than puff pastry. The pastry for the bottom should be thinner than the top to give it a better chance of cooking through. Put a baking sheet in the oven to heat up and put the filled pie dish on to it so that the base gets some direct heat, and cook the pie near the bottom of the oven, especially if it's a bottom heating one.

If you like the sort of pie with lots and lots of gravy, go for a top-pastry only option. To keep the top firmly on the dish, brush the rim of the pie dish with water or egg, and fix on a narrow strip of pastry to reinforce the edge. Brush with more egg or water and lay the pastry lid over, pinching the edges together well.

Whether your pie is single or double crust, a pie funnel keeps the top pastry lifted high so it doesn't get saturated with juices or sag unappealingly: kitchen shops sell plain white ones, adorably kitsch little porcelain blackbirds, or you can improvise with an upturned egg cup.

If making a double-cruster, keep the filling dryish or the pastry base will be soggy. If lots of sauce is needed, poke a funnel in the top at the end of the cooking time. Pour in a little hot gravy or (very French) a mixture of cream and egg yolks.

THE PASTRY

It's crucial that the pastry is thoroughly cooked. The oven temperature must be at least 190°C/375°F/Gas 5 to achieve this. Butter-only recipes have a fantastic flavour but lard gives a light, crumbly texture that's particularly delicious and very traditionally British. I choose a happy compromise of one part lard to three butter, which seems right for a meat pie.

THE FILLING

As for the filling, nothing is more disappointing than a bland pie. Be generous with aromatics (remember that show-stopping steam when you cut it open) and brown the meat well in a pan first to make rich juices. Chicken can finish cooking with the pastry, but red meat needs cooking slowly to tenderness before the top goes on. Sounds like a casserole? Think of a pie as a casserole with theatre.

GRAVY V WHITE SAUCE

The deep brown and savoury juices of a casserole are the perfect moistener, but for chicken and pork, consider a creamy white sauce (see page 178) instead. This is especially useful when making a pie with the left-overs of a roast. Flavour the sauce with chopped tarragon, chervil or parsley, if you like.

good pies to make

Casseroles

Just about any casserole makes a good pie, whether based on red wine, beer, simple gravy or white sauce.

Chicken and ham pie

Use the meat from a small roast chicken and 225g/8oz ham, chopped into chunks. Bind with a white sauce, enriched with cream if you like. Serves 4–6.

Beef and mushroom pie

Use 900g/2lb braising beef and add 140g/5oz fried mushrooms, left whole if small, otherwise sliced. Shitake mushrooms (halve or quarter them) have a good flavour.

Venison pie

Venison has the great advantage of not having to be browned before it goes in a pie. Mix 900g/2lb diced braising venison with 4 tbsp flour and a fat pinch of salt and pepper. Fry 200g/7oz diced streaky bacon and a finely chopped onion until golden, then mix in the venison, 600ml/1 pint stock (half and half stock and red wine is best) and 2 tbsp redcurrant jelly. Tuck in 2 sprigs of thyme and a bay leaf and simmer for 1½ hours or until tender. Tip into a 1.3 litre/2¼ pint pie dish and bake as page 106.

Chicken and tarragon pie ➡

Preheat the oven to 190°C/375°F/Gas 5 and put in a baking sheet to heat up. Peel and cut 3 carrots into grape-sized chunks. Take 2 skinned chicken breasts (or the meat from 2 legs and 2 thighs, or a mixture of dark and white meat) and cut into chunks. Fry the chicken in 1 tbsp olive oil until just turning golden. Scoop the pieces out into a bowl, add a little more oil and sauté the chunks of carrot until just softening. Add 5 tbsp mascarpone or crème fraîche and 2 tbsp chopped tarragon. Taste the mixture and season with salt and pepper, then add the chicken. Line a 20cm/8in pie plate or tart tin with shortcrust pastry (you'll need a 350g/12oz quantity, see page 124), leaving a 5mm/¼in overhang. Spoon the filling in, then top with pastry, turning the edges over to seal. Brush with beaten egg and sprinkle with sesame seeds if you wish. Place on the hot baking sheet and bake for 35–40 minutes until deeply golden. Eat hot or cold. Serves 4.

serves 6

2lb/900g fruit, prepared

13oz/400g (1 quantity) sweet shortcrust pastry
  (see page 125)

2 tbsp cornflour or ground almonds

3 tbsp caster sugar, or enough to sweeten
  the fruit

1 small egg and 1 tbsp sugar, to glaze
  the pastry.

a fruit pie

PREHEAT THE OVEN to 230°C/450°F/Gas 8. Put a baking sheet in to heat up.

PREPARE THE FRUIT, peeling and coring as necessary, and cutting it into largish
pieces. Lay out on a tray to air-dry (the fruit may discolour, but don't worry).

LINE THE PIE DISH AND CHILL. Roll out half the pastry to line a pie dish
(around 8in/20cm across). Roll out the other half of the pastry slightly more
thickly, large enough to cover the top of the dish generously. Then lay it on a
cold baking sheet. Cover both halves with clingfilm and chill in the fridge for
30 minutes.

FILL THE DISH. Toss the fruit with the cornflour or ground almonds and sugar
and pile into the lined pie dish – aim for a jolly hillock of fruit.

COVER WITH PASTRY AND GLAZE. Let the second sheet of pastry warm up a
little so that it is less brittle. Brush the edge of the pastry in the pie dish with
water and lay the second sheet over the top, pressing the edges together well.
Crimp them into a pretty frill with finger and thumb. With a sharp knife, slash a
couple of vents in the top for steam to escape. Brush with beaten egg, or just
egg white, and sprinkle with sugar.

BAKE IN A VERY HOT OVEN, THEN REDUCE THE HEAT. Put the pie on the hot
baking sheet and bake for 10 minutes, then reduce the heat to
180°C/350°F/Gas 4 and continue baking for 25 minutes, until golden brown.

how to make a perfect fruit pie

FRUIT PIES ARE THE EPITOME of farmhouse cooking: wholesome, delicious, mother-love on a plate. They speak of plenty, harvests and gluts.

THE PASTRY

Sweet shortcrust is the thing here. Make it either with all butter, for flavour and crispness, or with half butter and half lard, for a meltingly short, just-like-granny-used-to-make texture.

TACKLING SOGGY-BOTTOM SYNDROME

The eternal problem when making a fruit pie is how to avoid a soggy bottom. One answer is to cook the fruit first, so that the excess liquid can be taken off. This is the failsafe method, but it is unsatisfyingly fiddly for a dish that should be simplicity itself.

An alternative is to mix 90g/3oz ground almonds with 1 tbsp cornflour to about 900g/2lb raw fruit. Letting the fruit air-dry, spread out on a tray, for an hour or so first will also help keep it from exuding too much juice as it cooks. Don't worry that it discolours: the brown edges will disappear in the finished pie.

Finally, it's easiest to make a fruit pie with just a lid and no bottom at all. It is less heavy to eat as well.

THE DISH

A metal pie dish will help reduce soggy-bottom syndrome, since it conducts heat to the pastry better. This is especially true if you bake the pie on a preheated baking sheet – just put one in to heat up when you turn the oven on. Single-crust pies, of course, can be baked in metal, glass or china. Choose a dish that's about 2.5–5cm/1–2in deep. It's important that it isn't too deep. The fruit will collapse as it bakes, so it needs to be piled up well proud of the top of the dish, or the finished pie will have a sagging, concave top.

PASTRY TOPS

You want to keep the pastry lid firmly fixed down, or as it cooks and contracts it will pop open. This is easy enough with a double-crust pie, since the two layers can be firmly crimped together. A single-crust pie needs reinforcement around the edge. Roll out the pastry and cut strips wide enough to cover the edge of the dish. Brush the edge of the dish with water or beaten egg, then lay the strips around. Brush them with egg or water, then cover the whole pie with pastry and trim with a sharp knife. Crimp the pastry firmly together and bake as usual.

THE FILLING

Now, the filling. This is where you have to use your judgement. The amount of sugar needed will vary according to the ripeness of the fruit and its own innate sweetness. Even sweet fruit will need some sugar, perhaps 3 tbsp. Rhubarb and

sour cooking apples need much more. Bear in mind that stone fruit like plums and apricots become more sour when they cook, even if they are sweet raw. Don't forget the option of brown sugar: soft brown for a gently syrupy quality, muscovado for caramel flavour.

As for the ripeness, the best option is firm fruit that is on the cusp of ripeness.

The size of the pieces is also a matter of taste. I prefer largish chunks, which may need cutting with the spoon, rather than anonymous-looking bite-size pieces.

good fruit pies to make

Pear and blackberry pie ↩

Slice 450g/1lb almost-ripe peeled pears into quarters and core them. Cut the quarters crossways into pencil-thick slices. Leave on one side to dry a little and brown. About 30 minutes should do it and up to 6 hours is fine.

Preheat the oven to 375°F/190°C/Gas 5. Toss the pears with 450g/1lb blackberries, 2 tbsp caster sugar and 2 tbsp ground almonds. (Taste the blackberries. If they are on the sour side, you may want to add an extra spoonful or two of sugar.) Pile into a pie dish. I use an oval dish about 25x15cm/10x6in and 7cm/3in deep.

Make 400g/13oz sweet shortcrust pastry (see page 125), flavoured with the grated zest of a lemon. Roll it out so it is large enough to cover the pie and make an edging strip. Brush the edge of the pie dish with a little beaten egg. Cut a strip of pastry about a finger's width and long enough to go around the dish. Press it on the rim, and brush again with egg. Lay the pastry over and press it on to the edges. Trim with a sharp knife and crimp the edges. Brush with beaten egg and sprinkle with sugar.

Bake the pie for around 40 minutes until the pastry is crisp and browned. Serves 6.

✳ GOOD COMBINATIONS FOR FRUIT PIES

For these you need 900g/2lb fruit. The quantity of sugar depends on the sweetness of the fruit. Taste the fruit and sugar mixture: it should be on the sweet side, and positively sugary for stone fruit such as plums and apricots.
❥ Rhubarb and banana with brown sugar and a gingery pastry: add 3 tsp ground ginger to the flour when you make the pastry.
❥ Pear and blackberry: berries are better mixed with a firmer fruit, or they cook to a purée.
❥ Apple and blackberry or blackcurrants: but not more than a handful or two of the latter, since blackcurrants are intensely flavoured.
❥ Peach and raspberry: add a couple of extra spoonfuls of sugar, since peaches, like apricots and plums, turn more sour as they cook.
❥ Apple pie with sweet cardamom pastry or marzipan: add the crushed seeds of 6 cardamom pods to the flour when making the pastry; or top with thinly rolled marzipan instead – it will flavour the juices with almond.

serves 4

7fl oz/200ml crème fraîche

2 eggs

pepper (and salt if needed)

8in/20cm shortcrust pastry tart case, blind
  baked (see page 116)

about ½ pint/300ml filling (such as that for the
  quiche lorraine pictured here)

7fl oz/200ml milk

6oz/170g chopped streaky bacon,
  fried until golden

a savoury tart

PREHEAT THE OVEN to 180°C/350°F/Gas 4.

MIX THE FILLING. Mix the crème fraîche and eggs in a jug and season with
pepper. Add any other chopped or liquid filling ingredients. (If they are large
and solid – slices of goat's cheese, say – it's better to put them straight in the tart
case, either before or after the liquid mixture is poured in.) Taste the mixture
and add salt if necessary.

FILL THE TART. Set the prepared tart case on a baking sheet and put it on the
oven shelf. Pour the mixture into the tart case and close the door. (Filling the
tart this way means you can fill it right up to the top, without risking spillage as
it's transferred to the oven, but be careful not to burn yourself.)

BAKE for 25–30 minutes until lightly browned and just set, but still a little
wobbly in the middle. Serve warm rather than hot.

what you need to make the perfect savoury tart

SAVOURY TART, QUICHE – call it what you will – is one dish that is especially worth making yourself. Never mind real men, no one who cares about their food would want to eat mass-produced quiche. A homemade tart is all about crisp, light pastry, and a creamy, barely set filling, filled with fresh, well-flavoured ingredients. It makes an exquisite lunch or an elegant first course that feels special.

THE PASTRY

Good pastry is vital. Ready-made shortcrust pastry is convenient but can have a tell-tale texture and taste of cheap ingredients. Hunt out all-butter versions, or make your own (see pages 124–5) – it's not hard.

Puff pastry tends to puff up too much or not to cook through when it is in a tart tin. For free-form tarts on a baking sheet, however, it's perfect, since it puffs up around the edges to make a rim. Be aware, though, that the base has a tendency not to cook through and you can get disgusting raw pastry at the bottom of the tart. To avoid this, either roll puff pastry out very thinly (about half as thin as ready-rolled puff pastry), top with the filling, which should be fairly dry, like a pizza topping, and bake. Or, for runnier fillings such as those using eggs, roll the pastry out more thickly and score a frame around the edge with a sharp knife. Don't cut right through. Bake the pastry empty for 10 minutes, before adding the filling and finishing cooking.

THE TIN

Ceramic tart dishes are pretty but don't conduct the heat well to the pastry and it's impossible to extract the first slice neatly. Loose-bottomed metal tins are the thing. Matt black tins conduct the heat more quickly, but usually have a non-stick coating which eventually flakes. Shiny metal tins come in a huge array of sizes but will rust if not carefully dried after washing and are thin so don't always conduct the heat evenly. The best all-round tins are those made of sturdy, dishwasher-proof, matt, anodized aluminium. Silverwood (www.alansilverwood.co.uk) is a reliable manufacturer.

As for the size, deeper tarts have become more fashionable of late and many recipes call for a tin at least 2.5cm/1in deep, rather than the traditional 2cm/¾in. Obviously, it makes for more filling per slice. However, if your tin collection hasn't kept up with the fashion, it's usually possible to bake the same quantity of filling in a shallow tart tin about 10 per cent wider. Since the filling isn't so deep, the cooking time may be shorter.

EXPRESS OPTION

For a quick fix, ready-made tart cases are the answer. Whipping up a filling and baking it takes minutes and is low stress. Choose the case carefully, though, since many are heavy with cheap fat and will ruin a good filling. Marks and Spencer make some good ones, and Booths produce little cheese pastry cases which are quite yummy with a long shelf life, making them great store-cupboard standbys.

how to make the perfect savoury tart

THE KEY TO ANY TART here, is crisp, well-cooked pastry. Because the filling is a delicate egg-based one, the pastry should be baked 'blind', or unfilled, first. This is a faff, but there's no getting out of it. But don't panic – or stop reading: there are ways of making it easier.

TEMPERATURE FOR BAKING BLIND
For pastry to cook through properly, the oven temperature needs to be at least 190°C/375°F/Gas 5, so that the pastry 'sets' and crisps up before the fat has a chance to melt, making the pastry collapse. Unfortunately, this temperature is high enough to overcook an egg-based filling, making it curdled and watery. The solution is to bake the pastry first, then reduce the temperature and add the filling. Even for non-egg-based fillings, it's still the best way to ensure that enough heat gets to the pastry to avoid soggy-bottom syndrome. I always pre-bake pastry unless it's for a dry, cakey filling such as a Bakewell tart or a French almond flan.

BAKING-BLIND TECHNIQUES
The traditional method of baking blind is to cover the pastry with a sheet of greaseproof paper and fill it with real or ceramic baking beans. But this is far from efficient. The beans are there not primarily to keep the base flat but to stop the sides collapsing down. Being round, they don't stay piled up at the edges, and they are also poor conductors of heat and so stop the pastry cooking evenly. Scientific chef Heston Blumenthal uses old foreign coins instead which stack neatly and conduct the heat well. Delia dispenses with both paper and beans to bake the tart case, which is okay but risky with delicate high-fat pastries.

This is my preferred way. Take a sheet of aluminium foil as long as the circumference of the tart tin. Roll it into a long, loose sausage. Coil it around inside the pastry, pressing it firmly against the sides to make an inner ring. After baking, the foil band can be saved and reused.

TIPS FOR BLIND BAKING
❧ Use a loose-bottomed metal tart tin.
❧ Chill the pastry-lined tin in the freezer for 10 minutes – about the time it takes for the oven to heat up to 200°C/400°F/Gas 6.
❧ Put a large baking sheet in the oven to get hot – this will help the pastry base cook through.
❧ Forget baking beans. Use the foil sausage technique (see right) and prick the base well with a fork.

To bake, preheat the oven to 200°C/400°F/Gas 6 and cook for 10–15 minutes until dry and just beginning to colour. Remove from the oven, take out the foil and assess for cracks which will allow filling to leak out. Large fissures can be filled with scraps of raw pastry and the whole thing returned to the oven for 5 minutes or so. Don't worry about hairline cracks. Take the egg white left over from making the pastry and tip it into the hot tart case, brushing it over the pastry liberally with a pastry brush. It will cook on to the pastry instantly and seal it.

good savoury tarts to make

Onion

Slice 900g/2lb onions thinly and cook gently with a fat pinch of salt in a frying pan with 100g/4oz butter for 30 minutes, until melting and golden. Mix with crème fraîche and eggs, season with salt, pepper and mustard. Pour into a blind-baked paastry tart case and bake as on page 114. Serves 4–6.

Leek and goat's cheese

Slice and wash 4 medium leeks (just the white part, not the dark green leaves) and cook them in 100g/4oz melted butter until very soft. Arrange 3 x 1cm/½in thick slices of goat's cheese log in a blind-baked pastry tart case. Mix the leeks, crème fraîche and eggs, season, pour over the cheese and bake as usual. Serves 4–6.

Smoked haddock and spinach

Cook 200g/7oz young leaf spinach in a covered pan with a splash of water until wilted. Tip it into a clean tea-towel and squeeze out as much liquid as possible. Chop roughly and mix with the crème fraîche and eggs, plus 250g/9oz cooked, flaked smoked haddock. Season the mix with salt, pepper and nutmeg. Pour into a blind-baked pastry tart case and bake as usual. Serves 4–6.

Mushroom and thyme

Slice 170g/6oz shallots and fry in 55g/2oz butter until soft. Add 450g/1lb sliced mushrooms, a chopped clove of garlic and 1 tsp chopped fresh thyme leaves. Cook until the mushrooms are soft and any liquid that they have given off has evaporated. Mix in the crème fraîche and eggs, season and pour into a blind-baked pastry tart case. Top with the leaves from a couple of thyme sprigs and bake as usual. Serves 4–6.

Asparagus and Gruyère

Break off and throw away the tough ends of a 450g/1lb bunch of asparagus. Chop the stems (leave the tips whole) and steam until tender. Mix the stems with the eggs and crème fraîche and 100g/4oz grated Gruyère cheese, season and pour into a blind-baked pasry tart case. Scatter over the asparagus tips and another 30g/1oz grated Gruyère. Bake as usual. Serves 4–6.

Crab and Parmesan

Spread the brown meat from a dressed crab (weighing around 300g/10oz) over the base of the blind-baked pastry tart case. Mix the white meat with the eggs, crème fraîche, 30g/1oz grated Parmesan cheese, seasoning and a small bunch of chives, chopped. Pour over the dark meat in the tart case and bake as usual. Serves 4–6.

Courgette, pea and tarragon tart ❯

This bright green, dill-fragrant tart is deliciously spring-like. Don't leave out salting and squeezing the water from the courgettes. It doesn't take long and it stops the tart being watery.

Preheat the oven to 180°C/350°F/Gas 4. Line a 20cm/8in tart tin with shortcrust pastry (see page 124) and bake blind (see page 116). With a vegetable peeler, slice 3 courgettes (about 15cm/6in long) lengthways into ribbons. Put them in a bowl and sprinkle with 1 tsp salt, turning the ribbons so they are well coated. Leave to one side for 20 minutes or so, by which time they will be bathed in green brine.

Drain the liquid away, and put the courgettes in the middle of a clean tea-towel. Bring the corners of the tea-towel together and twist tightly so that all the juice is squeezed out of the courgettes. Heat 1 tbsp butter and 1 crushed clove of garlic in a frying pan, add the courgettes (now in a tight ball) and tease the ribbons apart. Cook gently, without colouring, for 5 minutes.

Beat a 200ml/7fl oz tub of crème fraîche and 2 eggs together, and add 100g/4oz cooked peas, a bunch of dill, chopped, and the courgettes. Taste and season with salt and pepper. Pour the mixture into the lined tart tin and bake for about 30 minutes, until set but still a little wobbly. Leave to cool slightly and firm up (about 15 minutes) before serving. Serves 4.

ENGLISH OR FRENCH PASTRY – VIVE LA DIFFÉRENCE!

English-style shortcrust pastry is made with some lard, usually about half the total fat, with the rest as butter. Sometimes the lard is replaced with 'white fat', solid hydrogenated vegetable fat, but this is best avoided unless there is a vegetarian to cater for. The lard gives it a very 'short', melting quality, but a less rich, buttery taste.

French pastry, sometimes called pâte brisée, made with all butter, is crisper and less fragile. This is because butter is about 15 per cent water, which helps the starch develop, making the pastry hold together more (though too much water, and the pastry will be tough). Lard and lard substitutes, by contrast, are near enough pure fat, so make for a shorter pastry.

Which pastry to choose depends on the dish. For me, an English pastry is vital for a proper steak and ale pie, where it crumbles enticingly into the gravy. But for tarts the biscuity quality of French pastry is supreme. It's also more robust, and better than English pastry for eating cold, when the lard can taste greasy. This makes it a good bet for a tart or pie that's being transported, for a picnic perhaps.

serves 8

4oz/100g ground almonds

4oz/100g butter at room temperature

3oz/90g caster sugar

1 egg

1 tbsp plain flour

1 tbsp kirsch or other liqueur

9–10in/23–25cm uncooked sweet pastry tart
  case (see page 121)

about 1½lb/700g prepared fruit

4 tbsp apricot jam

a squeeze of lemon juice

fruit tart

PREHEAT THE OVEN to 200ºC/400ºF/Gas 6. Put a large baking sheet on the oven shelf to heat up.

MAKE THE ALMOND FILLING. Beat together the ground almonds, butter and sugar. Mix in the egg, flour and kirsch. Spread the mixture over the base of the pastry tart case. Top with the fruit, cut-side down (if there is a cut side).

BAKE THE TART. Put the tart in the oven on the hot baking sheet and bake for 10–12 minutes until the pastry is beginning to brown, then turn the heat down to 180ºC/350ºF/Gas 4 and cook for another 15–20 minutes, until the filling is set and lightly browned. Let the tart cool in the tin.

GLAZE IT. To make the glaze, put the jam in a small pan with the lemon juice. Heat gently until runny, then sieve out the lumps before brushing the glaze liberally over the tart.

how to make a
perfect fruit tart

A FRUIT TART is one of the most appealing of
puddings. It has a sense of occasion and the
attractively retro look of something from the window of a Parisian *pâtisserie*.
Whatever people may tell you about the excellence of those professionally made
versions, all too often they taste tired and dispiritingly of the cardboard carton they
arrive in. Making your own is not fast food, but it isn't difficult and tastes sublime.

The most adaptable and dependable fruit tart is based on frangipane, an almond
filling. This has a couple of major advantages. First, every fruit I can think of is
improved by association with almonds. Second, the cakey quality of frangipane
means that it can be baked at a high temperature, so that the pastry and filling
can be cooked together. This is in contrast to a custard filling, which requires that
the pastry is blind baked first and this is a slightly fiddly process. It's worth it for a
perfect quiche lorraine, but it's not a route I'm going down unless I have to.

THE PASTRY
Pastry is key to a good tart. Crumbly, flaky pastry, made with lard or white fat and
so good in pies, is not right here. A crisp, biscuity texture and buttery flavour are
what we're after, so choose a rich sweet pastry recipe, one involving butter and
egg yolk. If it has to be ready-made, Dorset Pastry (available from Waitrose and
delis) makes the best one that I've had, or as a last resort roll out regular shop-
bought shortcrust on icing sugar instead of flour. Demerara sugar is another
option, which makes the pastry crunchy and caramelly but tricky to handle.

PREPARING THE FRUIT
Berries can be left whole. Stone fruit, such as plums or apricots, should be halved
and the stone or core removed. Large fruit, such as apples and pears, need
peeling and the core removing (a melon baller does this neatly). The fruit should
be nearing ripeness. Rock-hard plums and pears will not cook in time, while
overripe ones will exude too much juice and taste insipid. If in doubt, pears and
nectarines can be poached first, but plums and apricots will lose their shape given
this treatment.

THE GLAZE
A jam glaze makes the tart look shiny and cake-shop perfect, as well as adding
texture and flavour. Sieved apricot jam is the classic, but apple jelly will do just as
well. Best of all? Quince jam or jelly: Tiptree does one, or if you're lucky you may
find a jar of homemade on the WI stall at your local market.

THE TIN
Although round is the classic, it's worth investing in a narrow rectangular tin as
well. Long, slender tarts look rather chic and are easy to cut. A tin around
25x12cm/10x5in will fit this recipe.

good tarts to make

All these tarts are made with around 700g/1½lb prepared fruit and will serve 8.

Poached quince ➡

Peel, halve and core 3 or 4 quinces (a melon baller and a sharp knife will do this neatly) and poach them in a syrup made from 250g/9oz granulated sugar dissolved in 600ml/1 pint hot water. Simmer very gently until soft. Slice the quinces, leaving them joined at the stem end, and fan out on the almond filling. Bake as usual, then glaze with apricot jam, or quince jelly if you have it. Scatter with 3 tbsp chopped, bright green pistachios at the end.

Plum

Use 700g/1½lb halved and stoned plums and make the tart as the basic recipe, scattering with 4 tbsp flaked almonds before baking or the same quantity of flaked, toasted almonds at the end.

Apple

Peel and slice dessert apples (the number will depend on size and how you cut them) and fan them out over the top of the frangipane and add half a teaspoonful ground cinnamon or crushed cardamom seeds to the frangipane.

Apricot

Take 700g/1½lb halved and stoned apricots and make the tart as the basic recipe, arranging the fruit cut-side down on the frangipane base.

Strawberry, raspberry and blueberry

Bake the tart with no fruit, just the frangipane. Spread with whipped cream, or crème fraîche, or crème pâtissière (see page 191), and tumble the berries over the top. Dust liberally with icing sugar.

makes 1 quantity (enough for a 10in/25cm tart)

8oz/225g plain flour

a pinch of fine salt

4oz/100g butter

about 1 tbsp cold water

1 egg yolk (save the white for sealing or glazing the pastry)

shortcrust pastry

MIX THE FLOUR with a large pinch of salt in a bowl.

RUB THE BUTTER AND FLOUR together with your fingertips until the mixture looks like breadcrumbs. Beat the egg yolk lightly with 1 tbsp water.

STIR HALF THE BEATEN EGG INTO THE FLOUR MIXTURE and bring together, adding a little more cold water if necessary.

KNEAD LIGHTLY until smooth, then pat into a fat disc and wrap in clingfilm.

REFRIGERATE for at least 30 minutes. If the pastry is too hard to roll when removed from the fridge, allow it to come up to room temperature.

HOW MUCH PASTRY DO I NEED?
- 6in/15cm tart tin or pie lid – 4oz/100g flour, 2oz/55g fat, 1 egg yolk
- 8in/20cm tart tin or pie lid – 6oz/170g flour, 3oz/90g fat, 1 egg yolk
- 10in/25cm tart tin or pie lid – 8oz/225g flour, 4oz/100g fat, 2 egg yolks
For a top and bottom crust pie, use double quantities.

how to make perfect shortcrust pastry

HOMEMADE SHORTCRUST PASTRY is buttery and light, a vehicle for fillings and toppings but delicious enough to eat on its own as a simple biscuit. It's also very easy, and tastes incomparably better than ready-made. While only the really dedicated would attempt puff pastry or filo, there's little reason not to make shortcrust.

THE PROPORTION OF INGREDIENTS

The classic proportions are double the weight of flour to fat, bound with just a little cold water, or egg yolk for a rich shortcrust. A generous pinch of salt is vital for flavour and the pastry will still probably have less salt than in ready-made.

USING YOUR HANDS

You can make the pastry in the food processor and I often do. However, it's not as light as hand-made. Working firmly but fast is the secret. While it's perilously easy to overmix pastry in the food processor, hand kneading will make it pliable and easy to work with. Within reason, that is. Treat it like putty and it will become hot and fragile, and then tough when it is cooked. Too much water will make it tough, too.

ROLLING OUT

Make sure the pastry is warm enough to be pliable but not so warm that it is shiny and weeping fat. Dust the work surface very lightly with flour, and arm yourself with a long, flexible, metal spatula and a good, solid rolling pin. Put the disc of pastry on the work surface and put the rolling pin, lightly dusted with flour, in the middle of the pastry. Roll firmly away, then towards you. Don't roll off the ends: a little lip should stand proud front and back, or the pastry will be too thin at the edges. Slide the spatula underneath the pastry to loosen it and turn the pastry round by 90 degrees. Repeat until the pastry is about as thick as a £1 coin.

LINING A TIN WITHOUT ROLLING THE PASTRY

There are two other methods that work as well. Try grating the chilled pastry and patting it down into the tin, pressing it evenly into the base and sides. Or slice the cold pastry thinly and make a patchwork of almost overlapping slices, then press the edges together.

SWEET PASTRY

To make a sweet shortcrust, mix 60g/2oz caster sugar with the egg yolk and blend as usual. The sugar will inhibit the production of gluten in the pastry, so it can be handled a little more without getting tough. It will also brown more easily than savoury pastry.

BAKING

Cooking time will vary, since fillings slow down the transfer of heat. About 10–15 minutes is right for an empty tart case, and as long as 45 minutes for a filled pie. Be suspicious of any recipes which suggest baking the tart or pie at less than 190ºC/375ºF/Gas 5. This is the minimum heat necessary to 'set' the pastry before the fat melts and the pastry collapses.

makes 6–8 pancakes

4oz/100g plain flour (about 4 heaped
  dessert spoons)
1 egg or 1 egg and 1 egg yolk
8fl oz/225ml milk, or half milk, half water
a pinch of salt
2 tbsp melted butter, plus more for cooking

batter pancakes

MIX THE INGREDIENTS. Put the flour in a bowl and make a well in the middle.
Break in the egg and add a splash of the milk and a pinch of salt. Stir the egg
and milk, gradually incorporating the flour to make a smooth paste. Beat in the
rest of the milk: the consistency should be that of single cream, so add a little
more water or milk if necessary. Stir in the butter.

COOK IN A REALLY HOT PAN. Heat the pan until it's really hot. Brush the pan
lightly with melted butter, using a bristle or silicone pastry brush or a wedge
of kitchen paper. Ladle in the pancake mixture: a scoop that holds 3 tbsp is
about right for a 9in/23cm pan. Quickly tip the pan so that the mixture spreads
evenly over the base.

NOW TOSS THE PANCAKE. When the edges start to look brown and crisp,
loosen the pancake with a spatula or fish slice. Toss it over and cook for another
minute or two on the other side. Slide on to a plate and eat as soon as possible.

MAKE THE REST of the pancakes in the same way.

what you need to make good batter

KNOWING A BATTER RECIPE off by heart will stand you in good stead. With that set of proportions at your fingertips you can make crêpes, fluffy American pancakes, Yorkshire pudding, toad in the hole – even a classic French clafoutis: enough recipes to see you through half the week.

THE PAN

With any kind of batter dish, a high, even heat is key. For pancakes, choose a decent-quality pan, with a base that spreads the heat evenly. I use a cast-iron pan about 23cm/9in across, which is a bit heavy (I've built good wrist strength) but makes a great pancake.

SEASONING A CAST-IRON PAN

Chefs often choose light non-stick pans, but since non-stick never lasts in my kitchen, I prefer to season my cast-iron pan to give a natural renewable non-stick finish. Heat the empty pan with a good handful of salt and 2 tbsp vegetable oil until it smokes. Turn off the heat and leave to cool a little. Wearing oven gloves and taking care not to burn yourself, take a good wadge of kitchen paper and scour the pan vigorously for a minute or so, pressing down hard. Tip away the oily salt and wipe the pan clean with more kitchen paper. Don't wash it with soap from now on.

THE PROPORTIONS

I have tried various combinations of eggs, milk and water to a constant 100g/4oz plain flour to find the ultimate batter. A mixture of half and half milk and water produces a slightly lighter and toastier-tasting result than milk alone, while beer is too yeasty. Two eggs gives a very omelettey flavour and a rubbery texture. The gold standard is 1 egg and 1 egg yolk, which makes for a particularly silky texture.

SUGAR AND SALT

A pinch of salt is vital for both sweet and savoury pancakes. Sugar is optional for a sweet batter but it makes the pancakes brown very quickly and gives them a tendency to stick and burn. Too much sugar imparts a biscuity taste to the pancakes, so limit it to a teaspoonful or two, or leave it out altogether, especially if the batter is an all-milk one: the lactose in the milk makes them sweetish anyway.

BUTTER

Don't, whatever you do, leave out the butter. True, it'll settle unpromisingly as a slick on the top of the mixture, but you can stir it in before each ladleful. The butter does double duty here: as a lubricant, stopping the pancakes from sticking and also adding flavour to the rather bland mix. Using margarine instead of butter will make margarine-flavoured pancakes.

MIXING
Making the batter by hand is soothing and not difficult, but I admit to resorting to a handheld blender when I'm stretched. Theoretically that will result in a tougher pancake, since the gluten in the flour will be more developed than by the gentle, handmade process, but it's unlikely anyone will notice.

TOSSING
When you loosen the edges of the pancake, it should move easily in the pan. Holding the handle in both hands, jerk the pan sharply forwards, angling it slightly towards you, so that the pancake flies out and up, flipping over and back into the pan. Cook for another minute or two until it is freckled with brown. If it doesn't work first time, keep trying: it's quite an easy knack to pick up. The pan will need greasing only every third or fourth pancake.

TO REST OR NOT TO REST?
Giving the mixture an hour or so in the fridge before cooking will let the starch in the flour swell a little, thickening the batter, and allow any gluten that's developed when the mixture was beaten to relax, resulting in a tender pancake. But although it does make a difference, if there's a kitchen full of hungry children, it would be madness not to skip the resting and just to get cooking.

Best option of all is to prepare the batter the day before and decant it into an empty milk bottle in the fridge. That's as far as getting ahead goes, since the most delicious pancakes are eaten hot from the pan, although it is possible to make the pancakes the day before and refrigerate them in a stack with strips of greaseproof paper between each one. Reheat by wrapping the whole bundle in foil and putting in a medium oven until hot through, or just by giving each one a few seconds in a hot pan.

good pancakes to make

Spinach pancakes

I like to do this not so much for the flavour (although it does result in a mild spinachy taste) as for the reason that it gives the pancakes a pretty green colour and stops the whole pancake event from getting too beige. It also makes a very light pancake.

Cook a handful of spinach (100g/4oz) in a little butter until wilted down (or defrost a cube or two of frozen spinach). Squeeze well in a tea-towel to dry out, then blitz into the milk (or the made pancake mixture) with a hand blender, until pale green. The colour will deepen as the pancakes cook. Fill the cooked pancakes with more spinach (200g/7oz fresh young spinach, wilted and squeezed to get rid of excess moisture), mixed with 250g/9oz ricotta cheese, 2 tbsp grated Parmesan cheese and 100g/4oz sliced sautéed mushrooms or a small fillet (100g/4oz) of lightly poached smoked haddock.

American-style pancakes (aka griddle cakes or drop scones)

Use just the basic batter mixture, with less milk, to keep them thick, sugar to sweeten, and baking powder to give them extra lightness. A touch of vanilla essence gives the right all-American flavour. There's not much that Americans haven't tried adding to their pancakes. The most successful are those using fruit, especially blueberries, lemon zest (as well as, or instead of, the vanilla), and spices (notably cinnamon or cardamom). You can add any of these flavourings to whipped cream to eat with the pancakes.

In a large bowl, whisk together 100g/4oz plain flour and 1 tsp baking powder to blend them. Make a well in the middle and break in an egg and add a splash of milk and a pinch of salt. Stir the egg and milk together, then gradually incorporate the flour to make a smooth paste. Beat in 700ml/6fl oz milk, and finally stir in 2 tbsp melted butter.

Ideally, let the mixture stand for an hour, or overnight – although you can cook it straight away.

To cook, heat a non-stick or well-seasoned frying pan over a medium-high heat. Melt a knob of butter in it, and drop in tablespoonfuls of mixture, letting it run from the tip of the spoon for the roundest pancakes. When bubbles start to rise to the surface of the pancakes and burst, turn over carefully and cook for a minute longer on the other side. Keep the pancakes warm in a low oven, covered with a barely damp tea-towel, while you cook the rest of the mixture.

GOOD THINGS TO ADD TO PANCAKES

➤ Lemon and sugar: the classic.
➤ Apricot compote: spread each pancake with 3 tbsp apricot compote from a jar.
➤ Rhubarb: 3 tbsp poached rhubarb for each pancake. Add a few drops of vanilla essence to lightly sweetened whipped cream to serve.
➤ Mushrooms: 200g/7oz mushrooms fried until soft and mixed with 3 tbsp crème fraîche and 2 tbsp grated Parmesan cheese. Enough for 4–5 pancakes (you can also add 1 tsp chopped thyme to the batter).
➤ Nutella and sliced bananas: spread each pancake with 1 tbsp Nutella and top with half a sliced banana. Eat with whipped cream or ice cream
➤ Apples: put 2 tbsp apple purée and a dollop of (or 2 tbsp) whipped cream in cinnamon-flavoured pancakes – just mix 1 tsp of ground cinnamon into the batter.

good things to make with batter

Yorkshire pudding

I like one big Yorkshire pudding cut into wedges, with a soft centre and crisp sides. If you prefer small one-per-person puds, use a bun or Yorkshire pudding tin and divide the batter between the cups (in which case this quantity makes 12 muffin-tin puds or 6 x 10cm/4in Yorkshire puds).

Preheat the oven to 220°C/425°F/Gas 7. Beat an extra egg into the basic batter mixture. Put 1 tbsp lard, dripping or vegetable oil in a baking tin about the size of a hardback novel (say, 15x25cm/6x10in and 2.5cm/1in deep) and put in the oven to heat. It should be a metal tin, not china, which won't conduct the heat well enough. When it has heated, take it out of the oven and pop it on the hob and heat some more, until smoking. Pour in the batter and return to the oven. Cook for 25–30 minutes until puffed and deep golden. Serves 4.

Toad in the hole with roasted onions, sage and bacon ➡

Preheat the oven to 220°C/425°F/Gas 7. Make one quantity of batter, beating in an extra egg and 1 tsp chopped thyme or oregano leaves. Cut 2 small, peeled onions into eight wedges each, cutting through the root so that the layers stay together. Take the rinds off 3 rashers of bacon and cut the meat into pieces the size of a postage stamp.

Pour 2 tbsp olive oil into a metal baking tin about 15x25cm/6x10in and 2.5cm/1in deep. Turn the onions in the oil and scatter over the chopped bacon. Pop in the oven to roast for 10 minutes until the onions are soft and lightly coloured. Stir up the contents of the pan to loosen any bits which are stuck on the bottom. Roll 6 sausages in the fat, then pour in the batter, scatter over 6 whole sage leaves and return to the oven. Cook for 25–30 minutes until puffed and deep golden. Serves 2–3.

makes 1 loaf

1lb/450g strong flour

½ pint/300ml warm water

½ tsp yeast (dried but not easy-blend. See the conversions box on page 135 for fresh yeast)

1 tsp of salt

real slow bread

MIX THE DOUGH. Put the flour in a large bowl, make a well in the centre and pour in the water. Sprinkle the yeast into the water, and flick a little of the flour (a tablespoonful or so) into the water too. (This is food for the yeast, providing sugars for it to develop.) Leave for about 20 minutes, until the yeast mixture froths up. Mix the contents of the bowl briefly by hand or spatula, adding the salt.

KNEAD either by hand or by using a dough hook in a mixer. Return the dough to the bowl and cover with a tea-towel or clingfilm.

RISE. Put the bowl in a sheltered spot away from draughts. It should be at room temperature or slightly (but not much) warmer. Leave for 3–4 hours, until the dough has doubled in size. Punch the dough down, and shape it into a round. Put it in a greased and floured bread tin or baking tray. Cover again and leave to rise a second time until the dough has nearly doubled in size.

BAKE. Preheat the oven to 200°C/400°F/Gas 6. Bake the bread for 40 minutes, or until golden and hollow-sounding when tapped on the base. Take out of the oven, remove from the tin or tray and place on a wire rack to cool.

makes 1 loaf

1lb/450g strong flour
1 sachet easy-blend yeast
1 tsp salt
½ pint/300ml warm water

fast-fix bread

MIX the flour, yeast and salt in a large bowl. Make a deep hollow in the flour and pour in the water. Mix to a dough.

KNEAD by hand for 10 minutes or in a mixer with a dough hook for 2½ minutes. Gather the soft dough into a ball, put into a bowl and cover with clingfilm.

LEAVE TO RISE in a warm place for an hour or so, until doubled in size.

BAKE. Preheat the oven to 200°C/400°F/Gas 6. Knead again for a few seconds, by hand, then shape into a loaf. Transfer to a greased and floured baking sheet or loaf tin, cover, and leave to rise again. This rise will be much shorter, 20 minutes or so. Bake for 35–45 minutes until golden and hollow-sounding when tapped on the base. Cool the loaf on a wire rack.

what you need to make bread

TWO RECIPES and the same ingredients (bar a variation in the kind of yeast), but two very different breads. The first recipe is the one used by my husband (and the family baker) Richard and produces a perfect loaf, with a delicious complex flavour. The other is my quick-fix recipe for when I want to make pizza for supper or breakfast rolls. It does also make an acceptable loaf but not with the magnificent artisan quality of Richard's. You choose.

Understand the basic chemistry involved in breadmaking and it's easy to turn out good bread. There's plenty of reason to bother. Most shop-bought bread (with a few honourable exceptions) is poor quality, made by the Chorleywood processing method that produces a fast, pappy loaf. Homemade bread tastes better and there is plenty of anecdotal evidence that it is more digestible. Master the basic recipe and you can make pizza and focaccia, too.

The essential ingredients for bread are just flour, yeast and water, and then other elements can make a difference, such as salt, fats and sugar.

FLOUR
Always use 'strong' flour, which has a higher gluten content than plain flour. Gluten is the protein that stretches and forms a springy network that gives the bread its risen shape. When you're experimenting with different flours – wholemeal, spelt, kamut and so on, as I hope you will – bear in mind that varying starch and gluten contents will mean they may need more or less water to make the same dough consistency. Look at the sample loaf recipe that is generally on the packet to get a rule of thumb.

YEAST
The yeast acts on the sugars in the flour to produce carbon dioxide which, trapped in the gluten framework, forces the bread to rise. There are three kinds of yeast available, all of which produce good results. The most widely available is easy-blend or instant yeast, a relatively recent invention which is convenient because it can be mixed directly into the flour rather than added to the liquid.

Ordinary dried yeast, available in tubs, is preferred by many bakers since it is less processed. Stir it into a cupful of warm water to dissolve it first, then add to the flour with the rest of the water.

Real bread connoisseurs use the purest yeast of all, fresh yeast. It comes in large blocks of buff-coloured paste with a crumbly, fudgy texture, and can be bought cheaply from bakers and sometimes even the bakery counter at the supermarket. You will probably have to ask for it, as it is rarely on display. Buy it in small quantities (they'll cut some off the block for you), since it doesn't keep well, although it can be frozen, well wrapped, in 30g/1oz portions (enough for a 450g/1lb loaf). To use, put it in a cup with 2 tbsp water, and cream together with a teaspoon. Mix into the flour with the water.

PROVING YEAST

Modern yeast is pretty reliable, but it is a living organism which can die or lose power if poorly stored. In the Real Slow Bread recipe on page 132, the yeast is allowed to froth up, or 'prove' itself, before it is mixed in with the flour. If you are in any doubt about the quality of the yeast – fresh or dried (you don't need to bother with easy-blend) – you can also check its vigour separately. In a jug or mug, mix it with 100ml/4fl oz warm water and 1 tsp sugar. Leave in a warm place for 30 minutes or so until it froths up like a pint of beer. This 'proves' that the yeast is in good working order, and can be mixed with the flour, along with the 100ml/4fl oz water used in the proving).

DIFFERENT YEASTS

When adapting recipes remember:
4 parts of fresh yeast = 2 parts of traditional dried yeast = 1 part instant dried yeast.

WATER

Use warm water to keep the yeast happy (it reproduces best at around 35°C/95°F). Too cold and the yeast cells become dormant; too hot and they die.

The wetter the dough, the better the rise, as the water turns into steam in the oven, inflating the bread. So add plenty of water: a good dough should be very soft, and very sticky until it's been well kneaded. A mixer with a dough hook helps here.

SALT

Salt isn't vital, but it improves the bread's flavour, helps it keep better and also strengthens the gluten, making for a better rise. Salt inhibits the yeast from rising too, so don't add it to the initial yeast and water mix.

TIME

Time is an important ingredient as well. It's possible to get bread to rise fast by putting it in a very warm spot or adding extra yeast. But the bread will taste dull and yeasty. Time allows a myriad of chemical reactions to take place, producing subtle complex flavours in the finished loaf.

FATS AND OILS

A tablespoonful of olive oil or melted butter mixed into the dough helps keep the bread fresher for longer. In small amounts, solid hard fats like butter and lard will improve the rise. Large amounts of oil or fat – for example in focaccia – weakens the gluten, giving a cakey texture.

SUGARS

Many recipes suggest adding sugar to 'feed' the yeast. In fact, there are plenty of simple sugars in the flour to keep the yeast from going hungry. But a little sweetness in a loaf is very pleasant, especially in a wholemeal loaf, so by all means add a teaspoonful for flavour. It may delay staling as well, but go easy as too much sugar will inhibit the yeast as it rises.

how to make the perfect bread

KNEADING

Kneading does two things. It develops the gluten to make the bread springy and chewy, and it incorporates air, helping the loaf to rise. Kneading by hand is fun, if tiring. Think of it as a workout. Rise up on to your toes and use the weight of your body to pummel the dough first in one direction, then the other, for about 10 minutes or until it is noticeably springier and silky smooth.

A dough hook does a good job and has the major advantage that you can make a much wetter dough, which may be just too soft and sticky to knead easily by hand. But don't over-knead – 2 minutes at low speed is long enough.

RISING

This is when flavours develop, and the carbon dioxide produced by the yeast expands into the air pockets created by the kneading. Although recipes often exhort us to leave bread in a warm place, the airing cupboard or even the warming oven in an Aga, these directions hark back to a time before central heating and efficient insulation. These days, normal room temperature (around 21°C/70°F) is just right for a steady rise. Leave the bread in too warm a place and it will certainly rise fast, but the flavour will be less good. Conversely, dough left in a cold fridge will still rise. Although it may take 12 hours, the flavour will be great.

If the dough over-rises, which will happen if it is left too long, the gluten framework is stretched too far and the air pockets collapse, so the bread will be dense and heavy. Press the dough gently: it should spring back. If it doesn't, it's over-risen, but a quick re-knead will rescue the situation.

BAKING

Once the dough is in the oven, the pockets of carbon dioxide expand in the heat and the moisture in the dough turns to steam, so the bread rises further and a crust forms.

A WOOD-FIRED OVEN EFFECT

A traditional wood-fired oven makes the best bread of all, holding in the steam, which helps develop the crust, and cooking the dough at a high, steady temperature, unlike domestic ovens which have a temperature that fluctuates by as much as 30°C/54°F as the thermostat kicks on and off.

Recreate the conditions of a wood-fired oven by using a large cast-iron Le Creuset-type pot with a lid. Preheat the empty pot in the oven, set to its highest temperature. Make a very wet dough, one too wet to shape properly, and give it its second rise in a bowl. Scatter cornmeal or flour generously over the base of the extremely hot pot (this stops the bread sticking), then pour and scrape the dough into the pan. Replace the lid and put the pan back in the oven. After 30 minutes remove the lid and cook for a further 20 minutes. Turn out the bread and cool on a rack.

GOOD THINGS TO ADD TO BREAD

Any of these may be added into the dough before it rises:
❯ 30–55g/1–2oz wheatgerm – packed with flavour and nutrients.
❯ 3 tbsp sesame seeds (toast them first in a hot, dry pan) or poppy seeds.
❯ 1 tbsp honey, golden syrup, treacle or maple syrup.
❯ 2 tbsp extra virgin olive oil, walnut oil or avocado oil (which also gently colours the bread yellow).
❯ A handful of chopped, stoned black olives (not the ready-stoned ones, which are tasteless).

good breads to make

Pizza

Preheat the oven to 220°C/425°F/Gas 7 and put a baking sheet in to heat up. Make the basic dough using either recipe (see pages 132–3), adding 3–4 tbsp olive oil after mixing in the water. After the first rise, roll out the dough thinly into circles on baking parchment. Spread with tomato sauce and toppings and allow to rise for 5 minutes. Lift the baking parchment and pizza straight on to the hot baking sheet and bake for 20 minutes.

Freeze spare raw dough, ready-rolled into circles, on trays in the freezer, then stack in freezer bags. To use, take out of the freezer, put on the toppings and slap straight in the oven.

Focaccia

Preheat the oven to 200°C/400°F/Gas 6. Make a very wet dough using either recipe (see pages 132–3) and adding 100ml/4fl oz olive oil. Press out on a greased or parchment-lined baking sheet or into a shallow baking tin about 22x30cm/9x12in. Make lots of deep dimples in the dough with your fingertips, pressing right down to the tin. Drizzle over a little more olive oil, letting it run into the dimples. Leave to rise for about 15 minutes then bake for 30 minutes.

Focaccia with red onions and rock salt ←

Before putting the focaccia (see above) in the oven, press on the leaves from 2 sprigs of rosemary and a handful (about 55g/2oz) black olives (buy them stone-in and stone them yourself). Peel 6 small red onions, and cut each into eight wedges through the stalk end. Turn them in a little olive oil and arrange over the dough. Scatter with sea salt flakes. Leave to rise for about 15 minutes and bake as above.

Bread rolls

After the first rise, divide the dough into twelve pieces (a knife or scissors helps) and roll them into balls with the palm of your hand. Arrange on a greased baking sheet and allow to rise again. Dust with flour or brush with beaten egg and bake for 15–20 minutes at 200°C/400°F/Gas 6. Cool on a wire rack, covering them with a tea-towel if you want a soft crust.

PUDDINGS
& CAKES

makes 8

2 egg whites
4oz/100g caster sugar

meringue

MAKE THE MERINGUE MIXTURE. Beat the egg whites until they are stiff. Still beating, shower over the sugar a little at a time, until the meringue is smooth, thick and shiny as shaving foam.

SHAPE THE MERINGUES. Preheat the oven to110°C/225°F/Gas ¼. Pipe or spoon the meringue on a baking sheet lined with baking parchment. Allow a little space between each one.

BAKE THEM. Bake the meringues for 1¼–1½ hours, until dry and hard to the touch, and hollow-sounding when tapped on the base. Allow to cool in the switched-off oven, with the door slightly ajar. Store in an airtight container.

what you need to make a meringue

AIRY AND VIRGIN WHITE, yet frivolous and voluptuously curved, meringues are the Marilyn Monroe of pâtissèrie, innocent and sexy at the same time. They are nothing more than air trapped in a honeycomb of oven-dried egg white, but they are also the best vehicle for cream known to man. And they are, curiously prosaically, the default way of using up leftover egg whites.

THE PROPORTIONS
For every egg white use 55g/2oz sugar.

THE BEATERS
Purists will tell you that the finest foam is achieved using a hand whisk. They'd probably like it even better if we all toiled away with just a fork. But for this kind of pillowy-soft mousse, an electric hand-beater or, better still, a tabletop mixer are the thing.

THE BOWL
This must be generously sized, big enough for the egg whites to whirl around nicely, especially if you're beating by hand. I wouldn't use anything less than 20cm/8in across and almost as deep; 30cm/12in across is better, and vital for more than 6 egg whites.

Copper bowls are the traditional choice, since the metal purportedly reacts with the egg white to create more volume. Almost as good is stainless steel, then glass and pottery. Plastic bowls are best avoided since they are very slightly oily and any grease inhibits the egg white foaming. For this reason, whichever bowl you use, it should be scrupulously clean, as should the beaters. Some cooks wipe the bowl with half a lemon to cut any residual grease, but this isn't really necessary.

THE EGGS
I use free-range eggs. You must make your own choice as to which eggs you use, but remember that battery eggs can have a slightly fishy taint.

THE SUGAR
If using white sugar, stick to caster sugar. Granulated takes too long to dissolve in the egg white. Using soft brown sugar instead of caster makes a delicious buff-coloured meringue with a distinct toffee flavour. Or substitute about a quarter of the white sugar with muscovado or molasses. Bear in mind the usual rules with brown sugar, that it is more hygroscopic (attracts water more readily) than white sugar and so the meringues will soften much more quickly. I've made delicious meringues using maple syrup but even in an airtight box they go sticky in a matter of hours, and I imagine honey would have the same effect.

THE FLAVOURINGS

Flavourings can be added to the sugar at will – a teaspoonful of instant coffee, a couple of tablespoonfuls of cocoa powder, finely grated lemon, lime or orange zest, dried lavender flowers. Bitty flavourings like coffee granules, citrus zest or the lavender should be pounded with some of the sugar in a pestle and mortar first. The cocoa and other finely ground additions – a fat pinch of ground cardamom perhaps – can just be stirred into the sugar.

how to make a perfect meringue

SEPARATING THE EGGS

Egg yolk is the enemy of good meringue because its fat content will stop the white from foaming up. Separate the eggs very carefully into two separate cups, then tip the white into the beating bowl. That way, if some yolk gets into a white, you will have wasted only one egg, rather than tainting the whole batch.

If a tiny bit of yolk does get into a whole bowl of whites, don't despair. Fish out as much as possible with a piece of clean egg shell, then beat as usual with electric beaters (I wouldn't attempt this by hand). It'll take a bit longer, and won't rise quite so high, but it's not a disaster.

BEATING THE EGG WHITES

Assuming you are using an electric whisk, once the whites seem ready, give the meringue mixture a final beat by hand, since tabletop mixers, powerful as they are, do tend to miss a bit. Tip the bowl upside-down to check that there is no slippage caused by unbeaten egg white lurking at the sides.

If you are stuck without any electric helpmeets and are beating the egg whites by hand, put the bowl over a pan of barely simmering water and keep whisking, adding the sugar gradually. The heat will help the sugar blend in and the meringue to form. This is called a 'cooked meringue' and is a particularly stable meringue, whatever method you use to whisk the whites.

SHAPING THE MERINGUES

The prettiest meringues are made with one generous spoonful of mixture, scooped on to the baking tray with another spoon the same size. If it finishes with a little peak that curls round to a question mark, so much the better.

If you have many meringues to make, particularly if they are very small, it will be easier to use a piping bag. Find the largest one you can and stand it point-down in a tall jar or vase. Fold the top of the bag over the rim and push the bag open with your fist. Fill with the meringue, then twist closed. Hold the bag in both hands, using the right hand (assuming you are right-handed) to twist the end of the bag, forcing the mixture down on to the baking sheet, and use your other hand to guide the bag. No nozzle is necessary; in fact a sturdy freezer bag will do as a makeshift piping bag – just snip the corner off after filling the bag. Fluted nozzles will make your meringues look factory-made, which seems to defeat the object somewhat.

good things to do with meringue

Pavlova

This can be made with just the basic mixture, spread into a circle and baked as usual. If you are after a marshmallowy texture, add 1 tsp cornflour and 1 tsp white wine vinegar to a 4 egg whites quantity (so with 225g/8oz sugar). On baking parchment, spread it thickly – at least 5cm/2in deep – into a circle and bake at 130°C/250°F/Gas ½ for 1–1½ hours, until dry to the touch but still soft inside. Top with 300ml/½ pint whipped cream and fresh fruit. Serves 6.

Roulade

This uses the same mixture as Pavlova (see above), with the cornflour and vinegar. Spread out into an oblong about 2.5cm/1in deep and bake as for a Pavlova – an hour should be plenty. Then turn upside-down on to a tea-towel, leave to cool and spread with whipped cream and a filling of berries or lemon curd. Roll up from the wide end, using the tea-towel to lift the meringue as you roll it up. Don't worry about the cracks. Transfer to a pretty plate with the join of the roulade underneath and dust with icing sugar. Serves 6.

Hazelnut meringue

Fold 100g/4oz toasted ground hazelnuts into the basic meringue mixture and bake as usual. Good with raspberries and cream rolled inside: mix 250g/9oz raspberries with 300ml/½ pint double cream, whipped to a pillowy softness. Crush the raspberries a little as you go, so the cream absorbs some of their pinkness, and sweeten very lightly with a tablespoonful or two of caster sugar. Serves 6.

Floating islands

Soft little meringues on a custard pond, these are a neat way to use both the egg white and the yolk in one dessert. Just drop tablespoonfuls of meringue mixture into barely simmering water and poach until set on one side, then turn and poach on the other side. Scoop out and drain on kitchen paper – they can be made up to 3 hours ahead – and serve on a plate flooded with custard made with the yolks (see page 190). Using the basic meringue mixture (2 egg whites) this will serve 4.

Apple meringue

Cook 3 large Bramley apples (peeled, cored and chopped) with 6 tbsp sugar and a tsp of cinnammon to a rough purée. Top with a batch of meringue mixture (try making it with brown sugar) and bake for 30 minutes at 150°C/300°F/Gas 2. Serves 4–6.

Apple snow with cardamom custard

We ate fluffy, mousse-like apple snow often when I was a child, sometimes with custard but more often without, since it was a handy way of using up egg whites left over from making mayonnaise. It's good both ways.

Peel, core and roughly chop 2 cooking apples, weighing about 450g/1lb. Place in a pan with 2 tbsp water and cook, covered, until the apples collapse. Whisk the purée to get rid of big lumps, then cool, cover and refrigerate.

Separate 2 eggs. With an electric beater, whisk the egg whites to a soft peak, then add 4 tbsp caster sugar and keep whisking until the mixture is as stiff and dense as shaving foam. Fold in the chilled apple purée and keep refrigerated for up to 3 hours.

To make the custard, beat the 2 egg yolks lightly with 2 more tbsp sugar, then heat 300ml/½ pint cream to boiling. Pour the cream over the egg yolks, still whisking, then return the mixture to the pan and add the seeds of 4 lightly crushed cardamom pods. Cook over a low heat, stirring constantly, and without letting the mixture boil, until it thickens noticeably. Strain and refrigerate.

Serve the apple snow in small bowls with custard poured around. Little biscuits are nice alongside. Serves 4–6.

Rosewater and ricotta meringue cake ➤

Crunchy, chewy, creamy, soft and marshmallowy, this dreamy 'cake' is really a huge meringue. Rosewater adds fragrance and a subtle flavour, while the slight graininess of unsweetened ricotta stops the whole thing from being too cloying. Some fresh fruit – apricots, raspberries – layered with the filling tastes wonderful too. Either way, cut it with a sharp knife and eat with a spoon.

Preheat the oven to 140°C/275°F/Gas 1. Line 3 baking sheets (or 2 large ones) with baking parchment. Draw three circles 20cm/8in across on the paper, then turn the paper over – you should still be able to see the circles.

Whisk 4 large egg whites with an electric beater until they form softly drooping peaks. Still beating, add 225g/8oz caster sugar, little by little. Add 1 tbsp rosewater and keep beating until the mixture is as thick and densely creamy as a Mr Whippy ice cream. Divide between the three circles, dolloping it in the middle and spreading it out to the edges of each one. Bake for about an hour, until dry and firm to the touch.

Allow the meringues to cool completely before carefully peeling off the parchment. Store in an airtight tin for up to a day. A few hours before eating, mix 250g/9oz ricotta with 1 tsp rosewater, 300ml/½ pint double cream lightly whipped, and 2 tbsp crystallized rose petals. Use to sandwich the meringues together. Melt 55g/2oz white chocolate and drizzle over the top and sides of the cake. Scatter another 1 tbsp rose petals over. Leave in a cool place for the ricotta to soften the meringue a bit. This is rich, so serves 8 easily.

serves 4–6

4oz/100g butter

8oz/225g plain flour

4oz/100g caster sugar

1–2lb/450–900g ripe fruit, raw or
lightly cooked

crumble

PREHEAT THE OVEN to 180°C/350°F/Gas 4

FOR THE CRUMBLE TOPPING, rub the butter and flour together until the
mixture resembles coarse fresh breadcrumbs. Stir in the sugar.

SPREAD THE FRUIT IN A BAKING DISH. Cover the fruit thickly with the
crumble mixture.

BAKE THE CRUMBLE in the oven for about 40 minutes, until light gold and
crisp on top. Serve with cream, ice cream or custard.

how to make a perfect crumble

A CRUMBLE SHOULD BE a generous affair, bubbling and burning round the edges with toffee-sweet juices from the fruit that meld into the topping. And that topping, likewise, will have dissolved a little into the fruit beneath, thickening the juices and adding just a hint of uncooked biscuit dough to make a flavour that recalls childhood.

THE TEXTURE

A good crumble should be crumbly, with a sweet, gravelly topping just covering hot, tangy fruit. To achieve this you are going to have to get your hands dirty, or at least deliciously buttery and sugary, since the texture needs an unevenness that can never be achieved in a machine. A food processor will reduce the flour, butter and sugar to sand, which sits heavily on the fruit like a layer of shortbread. And never, ever, pat the crumble mixture down. It should sit lightly where it falls.

THE PROPORTIONS OF INGREDIENTS

The basic ingredients are fat, sugar and flour, but the proportions are less fixed than for a cake or pastry. Some cooks use equal quantities of butter, flour and sugar to make a very crisp crumble, good for sprinkling over cakes as a streusel topping. I prefer the softer, powdery quality of a 2:1 flour and butter mix. Cold butter gives the best lumpy texture.

STIRRING IN THE SUGAR

The sugar should be stirred in at the end, not worked into the butter at the start, which gives a too homogenous, biscuit-like texture. White sugar is fine, but brown has a richer flavour. Darkest brown of all, muscovado sugar imparts a smoky, autumnal flavour to apple and blackberry. My favourite is demerara, which has a pleasantly gritty crumble texture already and a light honey flavour.

THE FRUIT

Just about any fruit you like will work in a crumble, provided it is happy to be cooked. Defrosted fruit works well in general. Don't overwhelm the fruit with too much crumble. The hero of the dish is the fruit with the crumble adding texture and sweetness. Don't over-sweeten the fruit; the crumble is sweet, and you can always serve it with ice cream or custard instead of cream for more sugar.

TO COOK AND SWEETEN THE FRUIT OR NOT?

The crumble will have 40 minutes in the oven, which may well be enough to cook the fruit through. Nonetheless, it's safer to precook anything that is inedible raw, such as underripe pears or peaches. The texture is important, as is intensity of flavour. Berries and currants generally reduce to a mush, so something chunky, such as nectarines, say, will make for a more gutsy and gentler-tasting pud.

good crumbles to make

Peach and raspberry crumble

Preheat the oven to 180°C/350°F/Gas 4. Take 450g/1lb peaches. If they are ripe, simply skin and stone them. If the skins don't peel off easily, put the fruit in a bowl and cover with boiling water, then drain and peel off the skins before halving the peaches and removing the stones. Harder peaches will need poaching in a syrup made from 300ml/½ pint water and 225g/8oz granulated sugar (the syrup can be strained, cooled and used again for poaching fruit or making sorbet: store it in the fridge for up to 3 days).

Cut each peach half into chunks, spread in an ovenproof dish and scatter over a large punnet of raspberries (about 250g/9oz). For the crumble, rub together 55g/2oz butter and 225g/8oz plain flour to make a coarse crumbly mixture. Gently stir in 55g/2oz soft brown sugar and 55g/2oz chopped blanched almonds with your hands. Scatter the crumble over the fruit, and bake for about 40 minutes until golden. This is best with vanilla ice cream.

Apricot, apple and ginger crumble ◀

Preheat the oven to 180°C/350°F/Gas 4. Peel and core 450g/1lb cooking apples and cut into grape-sized chunks. Simmer 140g/5oz dried apricots (ready-to-eat ones are fine; I like the conventional bright orange ones for this) in just enough water to cover them until soft. Drain, then mix with the apple and 55g/2oz soft brown sugar.

For the gingery crumble, rub together 100g/4oz butter, 30g/1oz grated fresh ginger and 225g/8oz plain flour to make a coarse crumbly mixture. Gently mix in 55g/2oz soft brown sugar with your hands. Tip the apple mixture into an ovenproof dish and scatter the crumble thickly over. Bake for about 40 minutes, until golden.

Seasonal crumbles

❥ Summer crumble fruit: Cherries, blueberries, skinned peaches, apricots, early apples.
❥ Autumn crumble fruit: Pears, blackberries, apples, raspberries.
❥ Late winter or early spring crumble fruit: Rhubarb and banana, mango and lime with a coconut crumble.

GOOD THINGS TO ADD TO A CRUMBLE MIXTURE

❥ Porridge oats: substitute for half the flour.
❥ Chopped nuts: add 55g/2oz chopped hazelnuts, almonds, macadamias or just about any nuts apart from peanuts. Beware packets of chopped mixed nuts, which are mostly peanuts.
❥ Desiccated coconut: substitute for half the flour.
❥ Grated citrus zest: add the finely grated zest of 1 orange or lemon.

per person

1oz/30g good-quality plain chocolate
flavourings, as desired
1 egg, at room temperature, separated

chocolate mousse

MIX TOGETHER THE CHOCOLATE, FLAVOURINGS AND EGG YOLK. Melt the chocolate, adding a tablespoonful or two of strong coffee, liqueur or brandy per person if you like. Allow to cool to room temperature. Stir in the egg yolk.

FOLD IN THE BEATEN EGG WHITE. Whisk the egg white until just stiff, then fold into the chocolate.

POUR INTO RAMEKINS AND CHILL. Pour the mottled, unpromising-looking foam into 4 ramekins, and put them in the fridge. It will set to a smooth, deliciously dark mousse.

how to make a chocolate mousse

A GREAT CHOCOLATE MOUSSE shouldn't just be airy light. It should also have a sticky quality, like the best welly-stomping mud of childhood. You may feel a faint reluctance to relinquish the spoon and the suggestion of a squelch when you lift it out of the dark depths.

Darkness is important, too, as it is an indication that the mousse has been made with good, high-cocoa-solids chocolate. Look for chocolate with 60 per cent cocoa solids or more, one that melts smoothly on the tongue and leaves a lingering flavour in the mouth.

My recipe is based on the simple chocolate mousse in Elizabeth David's *French Provincial Cooking*. It's satisfyingly uncomplicated and makes a faultless mousse.

MELTING CHOCOLATE

Two things matter here. The chocolate must be kept dry as it melts, especially if you aren't adding any liquid flavourings, or it will go grainy (or 'seize'). It must also be heated very gently, since overheating will ruin it.

Break the chocolate into chunks, the smaller the better, and try these methods:
Melting in the microwave A 1 minute blast at 50 per cent power should do the job, but do check and move the bowl around each time, since a hot spot could easily scorch the chocolate.

A bain-marie Put the chocolate in a bowl and sit it over a pan of simmering water (not in it — the bowl must be larger than the pan). The problem with this method is the risk of steam getting in the chocolate and making it seize (see left). I prefer to cover the bowl with clingfilm, take the pan off the heat, set the bowl over the pan, and just leave the residual heat to do its work.

The oven The third option, and perhaps the best, since it's a dry and steady heat. Turn it on very low — no more than 110°C/225°F/Gas ¼, and less if your oven will do it — and put the chocolate in the oven in a heatproof bowl. Check every few minutes to see if it is ready.

Remember that if the chocolate is almost melted it can be taken away from the heat source and left to finish melting in its own heat.

HOW TO AVOID CHOCOLATE SEIZING

Few of us won't have experienced that dreadful sinking feeling when the chocolate, having started to melt so promisingly, suddenly goes granular. White chocolate in particular is prone to seizing. You can try saving it by beating in a little butter or flavourless oil, but here are some tips for avoiding the situation in the first place:
❥ Don't let the chocolate get too hot. It melts at body temperature (which is why it melts in your hand and your mouth), and if it rises above 55°C/131°F its structure may be damaged.
❥ Don't let small amounts of liquid (the steam from the bain-marie, or just a few drops of liqueur) get in. If you are adding liquid, make it at least 1 tbsp per 30g/1oz chocolate.
❥ Allow the chocolate to cool to room temperature before adding the egg yolks, which must also be at room temperature.
❥ Add a dollop of butter to the chocolate before putting it on to melt.

good chocolate mousses to make

FLAVOURINGS

For every 4 mousses add:

❥ 2 bulbs of preserved ginger in syrup, finely chopped.

❥ 1 tsp very finely chopped rosemary.

❥ A few drops of mint essential oil.

❥ The grated zest of an orange.

TOPPINGS

❥ A pool of cold single cream (especially if the chocolate is very dark).

❥ 1 tsp crushed praline scattered over each mousse.

❥ A couple of crystallized violets dropped on each mousse.

BAKED CHOCOLATE MOUSSE

Dredge each mousse with 1 tsp of caster sugar and bake at 200°C/400°F/Gas 6 for 6–7 minutes (not longer or they will toughen). Carry the puffed-up mousses to the table and eat them instantly with cream dolloped in.

serves 4

3 egg yolks
3 tbsp sugar
1 pint/600ml single cream
flavourings or puréed fruit, as desired

basic ice cream mixture

START BY MAKING A CUSTARD. Beat the egg yolks and sugar together. Bring the cream to the boil, then pour it over the egg yolks, beating all the time. Rinse out the pan, then return to the heat and pour in the egg mixture. Cook over a low heat, stirring constantly with a rubber spatula, running it tightly over the sides and base so that the custard doesn't overcook there. Don't allow the mixture to boil, or the egg will scramble, but it should get hot enough that you won't want to put your finger in the custard for more than a second and the mixture noticeably thickens.

STRAIN THE CUSTARD AND ADD FLAVOURINGS. Draw the pan off the heat and pour the custard through a fine sieve, then cool and allow to chill in the fridge. Add flavourings or up to 600ml/1 pint puréed fruit (less for strongly flavoured fruit like gooseberries) and taste for sweetness.

FREEZE. Churn in an ice-cream maker (if you do not have one, see opposite).

how to make perfect ice cream

ICE CREAM IS THE ULTIMATE crowd pleaser, especially when it's homemade. There are good ready-made ice creams available, but the fruit ones, especially, lack the fresh flavour of ice cream that is eaten within a day or two of being made.

THE BASE: CUSTARD
Just about any liquid can be churned while it freezes to make a soft, creamy texture. So there are a hundred ways to make ice cream. Flavouring and freezing cream is the most basic method. But really great ice cream needs to be custard-based. The egg yolks give richness without heaviness or greasiness and a particular silkiness to the final texture. The custard also provides background taste that rounds out the main flavour whilst being almost imperceptible itself.

THINGS TO ADD TO ICE CREAM

Put sweet, crisp-textured additions into the ice cream after churning, but only for ice cream that you are going to eat today, since most of these additions will soften too much overnight.
➤ Biscuits: bash up 4–5 shortbread biscuits and turn in 3 tbsp melted butter mixed with 2 tbsp brown sugar. Stir into plum ice cream.
➤ Amaretti: crumble 6 amaretti biscuits and add to apricot ice cream.
➤ Honeycomb: break up a Crunchie bar and stir into vanilla ice cream.
➤ Meringue: crumble 4–5 egg-sized meringues and stir into raspberry ice cream.
➤ Chocolate flakes: shave 4 tbsp or so from a bar with a potato peeler and add to mint and other ice creams.

NO ICE-CREAM MACHINE?
Freeze the mixture for 1–1½ hours or so – the precise timing depends on how cold your freezer and the mixture are. The ice cream should be frozen around the edges but still mushy in the middle. Scrape the mixture into the food processor and whiz until smooth. Return to the freezer for another 1½ hours and repeat the process. Freeze until firm, giving it another blitz in the food processor if it seems not smooth enough.

HOW TO MAKE A RIPPLE

A ripple can be added straight after churning when the ice cream has been scraped into a plastic box. If you are freezing the ice cream without a machine, choose a moment when the ice cream is holding its shape but not quite firm.

Trickle a ribbon of sweet sauce (chocolate or butterscotch) or of sieved jam (raspberry, strawberry or blackcurrant spring to mind) over the ice cream, letting it sink in if it wants to. I use about 6–8 tbsp for 600ml/1 pint ice cream. Stir the ice cream once or twice, trying to distribute the ripple with out amalgamating it. Freeze straight away.

good ice creams to make

Spring

Rhubarb makes excellent ice cream and its flavour is good rounded off with 1 tsp Pernod or by infusing the milk with a few crushed star anise. With a dearth of home-grown fruit, it's a good time to turn to the frozen fruit – your own, or even supermarket raspberries from the freezer cabinet make a good ice cream. Defrost them (about 300g/11oz should do it) and rub through a sieve to make a purée. Sweeten and mix with the ice cream base. For gardeners, peach leaves add a subtle almond fragrance, and the new shoots of rosemary have a subtlety that the plant loses with age: infuse the leaves in the milk or cream.

Summer

Summer fruit like strawberries and redcurrants make lovely ice creams. Blackcurrants are successful too, although their flavour is strong, so be careful, and add the purée to the ice cream base gradually. Gooseberries, like rhubarb, benefit from a little Pernod.
❧ Lavender ice cream: Infuse the cream with 2 tsp lavender flowers (some delis stock dried lavender for culinary use, or use unsprayed ones from your own garden) and 2 tbsp honey, or sweeten the custard with a ready-made lavender sugar (Hanbury Foods do a good one, available from delis and www.bartspices.com). ➥

Autumn

Apples, the stalwart of the autumn fruit bowl, are rarely strongly flavoured enough to take the dilution with milk and cream. Look to nuts, finely ground and infused in the milk, or pears instead. Choose under-ripe pears and poach them until soft, to stop them browning, rather than already ripe ones.
❧ Damson ice cream: Stew 450g/1lb damsons with 300ml/½ pint water until soft. Rub through a sieve to get rid of the stones and mix with the custard. Sweeten generously: damsons are sour. ➥
❧ Hazelnut ice cream: Toast 200g/7oz hazelnuts and rub off the skins in a tea-towel. Grind finely in a food processor, then add to the custard and liquidize the mixture until smooth with 90g/3oz soft brown sugar. Add 1 tbsp hazelnut liqueur, then freeze to a slightly grainy but delicious ice cream. ➥

Winter

Ice cream is just as good in the chill of winter. Ice-cream sellers in Moscow do a roaring trade even when the temperature falls well below zero – it warms you up, they say.

Spice is a good choice of flavouring. Infuse the milk or cream with 1 tsp cardamom pods, crushed so that they just split, or a couple of cinnamon sticks similarly bashed. Eat the resulting ice cream with apple pie or crumble, or hot chocolate sauce.

serves 4–6

8oz/225g granulated sugar
1 pint/600ml fruit purée
juice of 1 lemon

sorbet

MAKE A SYRUP. Put the sugar in a small pan and pour over 8fl oz/225ml boiling water. Stir until all the sugar is dissolved (check the back of the spoon to make sure there are no sugar crystals clinging to it). Bring to the boil and simmer for 5 minutes. Cool.

MIX AND TASTE. Mix the fruit purée with half the sugar syrup and lemon juice. Taste and add the rest gradually: the mix should taste just a bit too sweet and acid. Chill the mixture.

CHURN AND FREEZE. Churn in an ice cream maker (see page 163 if you do not have one), then, once the mixture is too stiff for the paddle to turn, scrape it into a plastic box. Cover with a sheet of clingfilm pressed against the surface of the sorbet to stop it picking up unwanted flavours, put on a lid and store in the freezer. Give it 15 minutes or so in the fridge to soften a little before serving.

how to make a perfect sorbet

A GOOD SORBET is the essence of the fruit, refreshing and mouth-filling. We should eat more sorbet. It is really quite healthy but it still feels like a treat.

THE FRUIT

Use roughly equal volumes of syrup and fruit purée. Just about any fruit makes a good sorbet and even delicate flavours work.

Strawberries and raspberries need only puréeing and sieving (don't forget the sieving: seeds spoil the smoothly sybaritic quality of ices). Currants and gooseberries should be cooked, in the minimum of water, until they collapse, before puréeing.

Any fruit which goes brown when cut will need cooking to destroy the browning enzyme – a brown apple, pear or peach sorbet is very disappointing. Peel and core the fruit, cut it into chunks, and simmer in some of the syrup, then allow to cool and purée.

PURÉEING

Although fruit can be bashed through a sieve, a liquidizer is faster and far more efficient. Or, and this is especially worthwhile in a kitchen short of storage space, a hand blender, followed by the sieve, will do the job.

GOOD THINGS TO ADD TO A SORBET

❥ An egg white, lightly beaten, lightens the texture and inhibits crystallisation – useful if the sorbet is to be stored for a few days.
❥ Gelatine, dissolved in a little warm water, makes the sorbet hold its shape better as it melts.
❥ Liqueurs and spirits add flavour and make for a softer texture, since the alcohol impedes the freezing process. Don't overdo it – no more than 1 tbsp or the sorbet won't freeze.

SYRUP

Sorbets are generally based on what chefs call a stock syrup, a single-cream- consistency sugar syrup. This is better than just stirring sugar into water, because it is assimilated more easily, but also because it is less likely to crystallize, making for a smoother texture. Be wary of using too much syrup, since it will inhibit freezing, making the sorbet too soft.

Taste as you add the syrup, though: if the fruit is ripe and sweet, it may not need it all. The mixture should taste just a little too sweet and too tart, with a slight syrupiness. If it is sweet enough, but you feel there is not enough syrup in to give the sorbet a smooth texture, a teaspoonful of liquid glucose (from cake decorating and kitchen supply shops) will soften the ice but add less sweetness than syrup.

THE LEMON JUICE

The tang of citrus is indispensable for just about any sorbet. Even sour fruit like gooseberries benefit from a squeeze of lemon or lime, and honey-sweet fruit like melon would be lost without it. Don't even think about using lemon juice from a bottle: it has a weird cooked bitterness which will transfer itself to the sorbet.

NO ICE-CREAM MACHINE?
Freeze the mixture for 1½ hours – much depends on how cold your freezer and the mixture are. The sorbet should be frozen around the edges but still mushy in the middle. Scrape the mixture into the food processor and whiz until smooth. Return to the freezer for another 1½ hours and repeat the process. Freeze until firm, giving it another blitz in the food processor if it seems not smooth enough.

good sorbets to make

Seasonal sorbets

❥ Spring
Rhubarb
Pineapple and mint
Passion fruit
Mango

❥ Autumn
Melon
Pear
Apple and blackberry

❥ Summer
Strawberry and mint
Peach and amaretto

❥ Winter
Seville orange
Lemon
Lime
Lemongrass

Intense chocolate sorbet

This is perfect for when it has to be chocolate for pudding but the rest of the meal is on the rich side. It delivers a big dark chocolate hit without much fat. Try it with a scoop of vanilla ice cream – though real chocophiles will want to eat it on its own.

Put 225g/8oz cocoa powder and 100g/4oz granulated or caster sugar in a pan with 225ml/8fl oz boiling water. Stir until the sugar is dissolved, then simmer gently for 5 minutes. Stir in 55g/2oz dark chocolate and, if you like, 1 tsp brandy or crème de cacao. Taste and gradually add 225ml/8fl oz more water, stopping when the flavour is right. Leave to cool, then churn in an ice-cream maker or use the method described at the top of this page. Serves 6

Melon sorbet ☚

Halve a medium-sized ripe melon (Charentais is especially good) and scrape out the seeds. Scoop the flesh into a liquidizer and purée until smooth. Add 600ml/1 pint sugar syrup. Add enough of the juice of a lemon to make a pleasant sharp-sweet contrast. Freeze in an ice-cream maker or use the method described at the top of this page. Serves 6.

serves 8

6oz/170g caster sugar

6oz/170g soft butter

1 tsp vanilla essence

3 eggs, at room temperature

6oz/170g self-raising flour

1 tbsp milk, if needed

just cake

PREHEAT THE OVEN to 170°C/325°F/Gas 3. Grease and line a 8in/20cm cake tin that is at least 2in/5cm deep.

BEAT TOGETHER THE SUGAR, BUTTER AND VANILLA ESSENCE until pale and the colour of clotted cream – you can do this with an electric mixer or in a food processor.

BEAT IN THE EGGS one at a time.

FOLD IN THE FLOUR. Do this by hand or the cake may be tough. Add any extras like fruit at this stage. If the mixture is very stiff, add 1 tbsp milk (don't add milk if there is fresh fruit in the mix). Scrape into the prepared tin.

BAKE for about 40 minutes until well risen and golden brown. Cool in the tin.

what you need to make a cake

SOMETIMES I JUST WANT TO BAKE A CAKE. Not a polenta-ricotta torte, or a chocolate truffle mousse gâteau. Just an all-purpose cake, one that I can add a cupful of fresh fruit to — whatever is in season — or make fragrant with spices or citrus fruit. This kind of cake is great eaten warm for pudding, served with cream, or as a teatime treat once cooled down.

The easiest formula to remember is the 'pound cake': equal weights of butter, sugar, flour and eggs (a large egg weighs in at about 55g/2oz). It makes a Madeira-type cake which is easy to experiment with.

THE FLOUR
Using self-raising flour saves fiddling about, but you can adapt plain flour by adding 1½ tsp baking powder to 170g/6oz plain flour. It should be ordinary flour (known as cake flour in the US) rather than strong bread flour. If it's a slightly nubbly texture you're after, replace one-third of the flour with polenta. Likewise, half or even all the flour can be replaced with ground almonds, for a moister, denser cake.

BUTTER V MARGARINE
It's often said that cakes will be lighter and more tender if they are made with margarine instead of butter. There is some truth in this. This type of fat can incorporate more air, and added emulsifiers make for faster blending, so less of the tough gluten is formed: that's why margarine is often recommended for all-in-one-type cake mixtures. But at what cost! Look at the ingredients list on the packet. Why would I bother to bake at home and then fill the cake with such artificial rubbish? And, even more pertinently, the cake will taste of margarine. Using butter gives a clean, buttery flavour and more than makes up for a very slightly heavier texture.

If you have other issues with butter, it is possible to make a good, if rather moist and dense, cake using oil, either a pure olive oil (not extra virgin — the flavour's too strong) or groundnut oil. Remember that butter (and margarine) contains a fair amount of water, so instead of the 170g/6oz sugar in this pound cake recipe, use just 175ml/6fl oz oil and add 3 tbsp water.

THE EGGS
Free-range and organic eggs generally come from hens with a better diet, which means that they taste better, without the dull or even fishy overtones of cheap eggs.

Adding fridge-cold eggs to the creamed butter and sugar is a recipe for a curdled cake mixture, and although adding flour may seem to bring it all together, the cake will be heavier than it might have been. It takes hours for eggs to warm up after a night in the fridge, so it makes sense to keep half a dozen in the cupboard instead; they'll last a week there. Otherwise, adding the eggs teaspoonful by teaspoonful can help maintain the lovely mousse-like texture of the mixture. And if it does curdle, don't despair: it'll still be streets ahead of a shop-bought cake.

THE SUGAR

Changing the sugar from white to brown makes a huge difference to the cake. Brown sugar is hygroscopic, which means it absorbs water. So cakes made with brown sugar don't just carry the caramel flavours of the sugar, but they will also get moister and denser over a couple of days. Brown-sugar cakes are especially good in autumn with apples or pears in the mixture. So bring on the soft brown sugar, the dark brown and the muscovado!

Bear in mind other sweeteners, too. Substitute one-third the weight of sugar with an equal weight of good-quality marmalade for a bitter orange cake. Or use half the weight of honey, although this will make the cake very dark, so it may be best to stick to cupcakes, which spend less time in the oven.

THE TIN

Tins matter, and not just the size. Poor-quality, flaking non-stick can ruin a cake, while thin, cheap metal rusts and gives an uneven rise and colour to the finished article. Buy some decent tins, which nest together neatly, and they'll last forever and give great results. Mermaid and Silverwood are brands to look for.

A NON-STICK LAYER

A cake that, when turned out, leaves half still stuck to the tin is enough to make a grown cook weep, so some sort of non-stick layer is crucial. Greasing the tin with a lump of butter and the butter paper is fine. Follow this with a generous dusting, first with caster sugar (swill a tablespoon or so around to adhere to all sides, and tip out the excess) and then do the same with flour, to make a light, delicious crust on the outside of the cake. Alternatively, brush out the tin with oil – but be sure to use a mild, flavourless oil like almond or groundnut.

Lining the tin instead makes good sense, especially for cakes that are going to spend a long time in the oven, since the chosen lining provides an extra layer of protection against burning. I keep ready-made paper liners in the kitchen drawer (Lakeland Limited does a great range).

STORAGE

Any cake made with fresh fruit will need to be kept in the fridge, or it'll quickly turn mouldy. Other cakes are best kept at room temperature. To ward off staleness, a container must have a really good airtight seal, made of rubber or plastic, which is why plastic boxes are often more reliable than tins, if less charming to look at.

GOOD TOPPINGS FOR CAKES

It's not all about fondant icing…

❥ Crumble topping: Before the cake goes in the oven, sprinkle over a crumble topping made by rubbing together 55g/2oz each of sugar, flour and butter and ½ tsp ground cinnamon.

❥ Honey and demerara: Mix 2 tbsp honey with 2 tbsp demerara sugar. Spread over the cake while it is still warm.

❥ Lemon or orange drizzle: Hard to beat. Mix the juice of 2 lemons or 4 Seville oranges (use the grated zest in the cake mixture) with 100g/4oz caster sugar. Pierce the top of the cake with a skewer while it is still warm and drizzle over the sugar/juice mix.

good things to make with a cake mixture

Summer tart

Bake the basic cake mixture in the base of a 25cm/10in loose-bottomed tart tin lined with baking parchment, for 30 minutes. Cool in the tin, then lift it out on to a serving dish. Mix together 250g/9oz each of ricotta and mascarpone cheeses, 2 tsp vanilla essence, 1 tbsp caster sugar and a squeeze of lemon juice. Taste and add a little more sugar or lemon juice if necessary: it should taste neither lemony-sharp nor cloyingly sweet. Spread over the tart base. Pile at least 3 punnets of soft fruit (a mixture of raspberries, blueberries, redcurrants, blackberries, what you will, about 450g/1lb) on top. Trickle with 3–4 tbsp runny honey if you like. Serve as a pudding with a spoon and fork. Serves 8.

Cupcakes

Line one or two bun tins with 18 paper cupcake-cases. Drop dollops of the cake mixture into the middle of each case. Take care not to get any mixture on the sides, where it would burn. Bake in a hotter oven than for a large cake – 180°C/350°F/Gas 4 – for 10 minutes or so, until the cakes are golden and springy to the touch. Makes 18.

Traybake

Bake the cake mixture in a 22x22cm/9x9in tin, or one of a similar size. Lemon drizzle is eternally popular: add the finely grated zest of 2 lemons to the mixture before baking. Mix the juice with 5 tbsp icing sugar and spoon over the still warm cake, poking a few holes in it with a skewer to help the syrup soak in. Serves 8.

Upside-down cake

Use a non-loose-bottomed cake tin or a suitably sized ovenproof saucepan. Line the base with a circle of baking parchment. Melt 2 tbsp butter with 2 tbsp dark brown sugar and pour into the tin. Arrange sliced fruit prettily over the top: nectarines, apples or pineapple. Pour over the cake mixture and bake as usual. Serves 8.

Eve's pudding

Put about 450g/1lb stewed and sweetened cooking apples in an ovenproof dish (about 20x25cm/8x10in). Spread the cake mixture over the top. Bake as usual. Serves 8.

Sandwich cake

Divide the basic cake mixture between two 20cm/8in tins and bake in a hotter oven (190°C/375°F/Gas 5) for 20 minutes, until springy and pulling away from the edges of the tin. Fill with jam (it's the perfect way to make the most of homemade preserves) and, for real decadence, softly whipped cream as well. Serves 8.

Raspberry and lemon curd cake ➥

Lemon curd, splodged on top of the cake mixture rather than beaten in, bakes to fudgey, citrussy pockets in a raspberry speckled cake. Eat it for tea, or as a pudding with créme fraîche. It's easy: spread the basic cake mixture out in the usual tin. Dollop with whole teaspoonfuls of lemon curd (about half a 450g/1lb jar) and scatter a handful of raspberries over the top. Bake as usual. Serves 8.

Chocolate cake

The perfect chocolate cake is a holy grail, but its exact form depends partly on what you're after. For a standard chocolate cake to ice for a children's party or for a traybake, substitute 4 tbsp of the flour in the basic cake recipe with cocoa powder, and use dark brown sugar. For a grown-up, rich chocolate torte, use the following recipe that has ground almonds instead of flour and adds 70 per cent cocoa solids chocolate, melted into the butter.

Preheat the oven to 190°C/375°F/Gas 5. Line a 20cm/8in cake tin with baking parchment.

Melt 200g/7oz each of unsalted butter and plain chocolate together, either in the microwave or in a bowl placed over a pan of hot water. Stir in 5 large egg yolks and 200g/7oz ground almonds. Whisk 5 large egg whites until they form soft peaks, then whisk in 200g/7oz caster sugar, a little at a time, to make a stiff, shiny foam. Fold the chocolate and egg white mixtures together and scrape into the cake tin. Bake for 40 minutes, then cover the cake with a piece of baking parchment to stop it getting too dark, and bake for another 10–20 minutes until well risen and firm to the touch. Cool in the tin.

If you feel this simple cake needs tarting up a bit, and sometimes I do, cover it with a slick of melted chocolate and scatter with crystallized violets. Serves 10.

❊ SEASONAL CAKES

Adding things to cakes is lovely. Bear in mind that the mixture must be dense enough to hold up the bits, so keep it to a stiff dropping consistency: that's to say a spoonful should fall off the spoon only when given a sharp jerk. When adding large quantities of juicy berries, which will leak lots of juice in the heat of the oven, adding an extra 2 tbsp flour makes the cake easier to slice.

❦ **Summer**
A handful of blackcurrants, redcurrants, small gooseberries or raspberries.
A tablespoon of rosewater and a handful of crystallized rose petals.

❦ **Winter**
A couple of peeled, finely sliced apples and 1 tsp ground cinnamon.
A peeled, chopped pear and 2 tsp ground ginger.
A couple of sticks of forced rhubarb, chopped, and a handful of chopped dates.

makes 20–25

4oz/100g butter
2oz/55g caster sugar
5oz/140g plain flour

fork biscuits

PREHEAT THE OVEN AND PREPARE A BAKING SHEET. Preheat the oven
to 180°C/350°F/Gas 4. Grease a large baking sheet or line it with
baking parchment.

MIX THE INGREDIENTS. Beat the butter and sugar together until pale and fluffy.
Sift over the flour and blend in. Bring the mixture together and knead lightly to
make a cohesive dough.

ROLL THE DOUGH INTO BALLS and arrange, well-spaced, on the baking sheet.
Press each ball down gently with the tines of a fork.

BAKE for 10–15 minutes until light golden brown. Allow to 'set' on the baking
sheet for a couple of minutes, then lift on to a rack to finish cooling.

how to make perfect biscuits

THERE ARE SO MANY BISCUITS, and so many biscuit lovers, that I wouldn't presume to tell you which recipe is definitive. You may already know your own biscuit perfection. It may even come in a packet. But just in case you need to rustle up a tray of sweet-smelling, fresh-baked cookies, here's a know-by-heart recipe.

THE INGREDIENTS

Biscuits are nothing if not temperamental. Quite small alterations in the proportion of flour, butter and sugar make a big difference to the softness, crispness and shortness of the biscuit. So does how long the biscuit is left in the oven. Those soft, doughy American cookies are deliberately undercooked to give them their characteristic softness, while a gingernut must be baked long enough to turn snappily crisp when bitten.

❥ More butter will make the biscuit 'shorter': that is, more crumbly and melt-in-the-mouth. The flavour will be apparent, so I wouldn't use margarine, even though it makes the biscuit even shorter. The soft-spread butter in tubs is best avoided too since the chemical make-up can vary from brand to brand.

❥ More sugar makes for a crisper biscuit.

❥ Egg, in small amounts, will give a cakey consistency and stop the biscuit from spreading so much as it bakes.

❥ Golden syrup gives chewiness.

❥ Cornflour also makes the biscuit shorter.

GOOD THINGS TO ADD TO FORK (OR SHORTBREAD) BISCUITS

❥ Chocolate: Replace 2 tbsp of the flour with 2 tbsp cocoa powder. Especially good drizzled with melted white chocolate.

❥ Chocolate chips: Mix in 30g/1oz chocolate chips.

❥ Rosemary: The leaves from a young sprig, chopped, make the biscuits intriguing and delicious.

❥ Lavender: Add 2 tsp dried lavender flowers, or replace the sugar with lavender sugar.

❥ Ginger: Mix in 1 tsp ground ginger and 2 bulbs of chopped stem ginger in syrup.

❥ Fennel seed: Add 1 tsp for a gentle aniseed flavour.

❥ Crystallized rose petals: Stir in 1 tbsp for colour and crunch – or drizzle the biscuits with white icing and sprinkle over rose petals.

THE OVEN

With all that sugar, biscuits burn in a blink. If your oven doesn't heat evenly, some will darken too much before others are done, so turn the baking sheet at least once during baking to even things up. A good quality, heavyweight baking sheet will help here. Mine are made by Silverwood, and are so solid they'll probably still serve my grandchildren well.

THE DOUGH

As with pastry, it's important not to overwork the dough. While the sugar will inhibit the development of gluten (which is what makes pastry tough) you don't want to make the butter melt to oil, or the dough will be hard to handle.

good biscuits to make

Shortbread biscuits

Rolling the dough and then chilling it makes it easy to stamp out with a biscuit cutter. Just add another 30g/1oz flour – or cornflour, which makes the biscuits especially crisp and melting.

Prepare the dough as for fork biscuits. Roll the dough between two sheets of clingfilm, to about pencil thickness. Lift on to a tray and chill for 30 minutes or up to a day, still covered in clingfilm. Peel off the clingfilm and stamp out shapes with cutters. Lift on to a lined baking sheet and bake for about 10–15 minutes until set but not coloured.

Crunchy biscuits

The ingredients are the same as for the basic biscuits but adding golden syrup makes a crunchy-style end product and the bicarbonate of soda makes them puff up. You can add 1 tsp ground ginger with the flour, as well, if you want a gingernut.

Heat 100g/4oz golden syrup in a small pan and stir in 55g/2oz butter and 90g/3oz sugar until smooth. Sift over 170g/6oz flour and ½ tsp bicarbonate of soda and mix. Shape as for fork biscuits. Cook for 20–25 minutes. Allow to cool for a couple of minutes, then use a fish slice or metal spatula to lift the still-soft biscuits on to a rack to cool and firm up.

Jammy dodgers ➡

Stamp out pairs of shapes from the basic dough with biscuit cutters, then stamp a miniature shape out of the centre of one from each pair. Bake, cool, then sandwich together with jam (sieve or blend it first if it is chunky) or lemon curd. Or Nutella, even, if you want to be very popular.

Cheesy biscuits

Rich and very crumbly, cheese biscuits have more butter in as well as cheese. Eat them with drinks before dinner.

Preheat the oven to 180°C/350°F/Gas 4. Mix 100g/4oz each of butter, plain flour and grated strong cheese – Gruyère or Cheddar, say – to a paste in the food processor, seasoning with a good teaspoonful of English mustard and a little salt if necessary. Roll into a log, wrap in clingfilm and chill. If you like, brush the log with beaten egg and roll in seeds (sesame, poppy, fennel, caraway), then cut into slices as thick as a £1 coin. Bake for 5 minutes.

SAUCES

gravy

*makes enough for a roast
for 5–6*

1 roasting tin with the
  roast meat in it
½ pint/300ml water
  or stock
1 tbsp flour
salt and pepper

REMOVE THE MEAT AND ANY VEGETABLES from the roasting tin and put the meat in a warm place to rest.

DEGLAZE THE PAN. Put the tin over a medium heat. Tip the water or stock into the pan and stir vigorously to scrape up the gunk from the base. Pour the resulting brown juices into a gravy-separating jug (or a bowl). The fat will rise to the top.

BROWN THE FLOUR. Return the empty roasting tin to the hob and add a tablespoonful of the fat now sitting on top of the juices. Add the flour and stir until it turns golden and smells nutty.

ADD THE JUICES AND STIR. Pour in the juices, leaving the fat behind (spoon it off first as best you can, if the juices are in a bowl), and stir until the gravy thickens. Simmer for a minute or two, adding more water or stock until it reaches the right consistency. Taste and adjust the seasoning.

how to make perfect gravy

AAAAAAAHHH, GRAVY! It just isn't Sunday lunch without it. And, truthfully, a flavoursome gravy can rescue a dull piece of meat. Good and hot, it can also make up for a piece of meat that has been left to rest for so long it's no more than tepid. And it can even make the driest turkey breast moist enough to enjoy.

The downside is that gravy is not the easiest thing to make. It's the timing that is all wrong. Just at the final countdown to the meal, when the vegetables need attention and the family has to be gathered to the table, and all the forgotten details need attending to, there's a hot roasting tin, spitting with fat and unpromising-looking brown gunk to be transformed into an appetizing caramel-coloured liquor.

Fear not. It can be done. I was against adding flour, thinking it was a cheat and that restaurant-style heavily reduced stocks were the answer, but then came to see that it's a key ingredient. The secret is to let the fat and flour cook to a nut-brown colour before adding the liquid. This adds subtle flavour and colour, as well as removing any gloopy quality. No more Sunday stress for me.

A DECENT ROASTING TIN
Start at the beginning. A good solid roasting tin will last forever. Crucially, it can be put on the hob like a saucepan, so all the delicious gunk that forms the basis of a good gravy can be dissolved into the water or stock.

THE VEGETABLES

What you roast your meat with will characterize your gravy. A couple of carrots and onions in the pan will help boost the gravy, and will taste good in their own right. A sprig or two of rosemary, the same of thyme and a few cloves of unpeeled garlic, will all add fragrance and flavour to meat and gravy.

A SEPARATOR

A decent gravy separator is a lifesaver here, because it's by far the most efficient way to get rid of the fat. Choose a large one, like Good Grips brand, or one in heatproof glass.

WHEN TO ABANDON SHIP

Sometimes the tin will be just too burnt, and there is nothing for it but to give up. If you are in doubt, splash water in the tin and taste the juices. If they taste dull, that's fine (it's not yet seasoned, after all). But if they taste burnt, the game is up.

EMERGENCY RATIONS

If I'm lucky, a rummage in the freezer will turn up a pot of gravy left from a previous meal, which I've saved to add to casseroles or to enrich future gravies. Failing that, bring on the redcurrant jelly, the cranberry sauce and the horseradish sauce, or some mustard mixed with crème fraîche and gently heated through.

good things to add to gravy

IF IT IS TOO SHARP

➤ Whisk in some butter over a gentle heat.
➤ Add a tiny pinch of bicarbonate of soda, but go easy or you'll get a soapy flavour.
➤ Salt can balance acidity.

IF IT IS INSIPID

➤ Simmer a sprig of thyme or rosemary in the tin – the flavour transfers quickly, so fish it out when the gravy tastes right.
➤ A slosh of Madeira or Marsala is worth considering, but boil them up in a separate pan first and hold a match to the vapour so that it flambés, which will help reduce excessive acidity.
➤ Heavily reduced stock or *glace de viande* is great if you have it. To make, boil homemade stock until syrupy, then freeze it in ice cube trays and add a cube to the gravy when wanted.
➤ A dab of Bovril is a cheat's way to boost a beef gravy, but too much will be overpowering.
➤ Surprisingly perhaps, a pinch of coffee granules can round out flavours.

white sauce

makes 1/3 pint/200ml

½ pint/300ml milk

½ onion, peeled and stuck
   with a clove

1 bay leaf

1oz/30g butter

1oz/30g flour

salt and pepper

INFUSE THE MILK. Pour the milk into a pan and add the clove-spiked onion and bay leaf. Bring to the boil, then put to one side to infuse.

MAKE THE ROUX. In a small pan, melt the butter and stir in the flour (this is called making a roux). Cook gently for a minute or so.

ADD THE MILK GRADUALLY. Splash the milk in little by little, stirring madly all the time. Once all the milk is amalgamated, the sauce should be smooth – give it a good whisk if there are any lumps. Season.

SIMMER the sauce for as long as you've got – at least a couple of minutes, but you can cook it for up to 2 hours on the lowest heat. Use a heat diffuser on the warming plate of an Aga, or it will catch on the bottom.

how to make a perfect white sauce

IT'S HARD TO SETTLE on which recipe is the most important to know by heart: which will improve one's cooking life most dramatically? It might just be white sauce. Whatever the consistency, it is the base for countless dishes, from macaroni cheese to soufflés.

THE SCIENCE BIT
The smooth, creamy texture is achieved by making sure that the starch granules in the flour don't stick together before they swell up and thicken the sauce. Coating the flour in fat ensures that they are well dispersed, and adding the hot milk gradually keeps things smooth. It's the protein in the wheatflour that makes it sticky. Cornflour has almost no protein in it, so will make a smooth sauce without fat. Simply mix the flour with a little cold water and then add it to the hot milk.

THE FAT
So, technically it's possible to make a sauce without fat. But that fat makes the sauce feel creamier and silky smooth. Oil, lard or margarine would work, but butter gives the right flavour.

THE MILK
Heating the milk first with half an onion stuck with a clove and a bay leaf gives it a subtle flavour, and, like a good stock, gives backbone to the dish. Sometimes, rushing to make supper for hungry children, or out of plain idleness, I use cold milk. The sauce still thickens, the dish still 'works'. It just isn't quite as good as it might have been. The major advantage of using cold milk is that it can be added

all in one go and whisked as it heats gently. The gradual rise in temperature allows those starch molecules to swell without clumping together. But if you do go down this route, add a bay leaf to the sauce as it simmers, to round out the flavour.

THE CONSISTENCY

You will need to judge and adjust the consistency of your sauce, adding more liquid to thin it or simmering to thicken it. Frustrating though it may be, a recipe can never tell you exactly how to get a precise consistency. There are too many variables: the size of the pan, the heat of the cooker, the quality of the flour. But you tend to make white sauce in the same pan, in the same place and with the same ingredients, so it won't take long to work out how to make the perfect white sauce in your way.

NAME THAT SAUCE

❯ A flour and butter mixture is a roux.
❯ White sauce made with milk is a béchamel.
❯ White sauce made with stock is a velouté.

STORAGE

A white sauce will keep for a couple of days in a lidded plastic box in the fridge. It will go solid, so when the time comes to use it, heat it gently in a pan or microwave, with a splash of milk to soften it.

good things to do with white sauce

White sauce is the basis of countless recipes, including gratins (see pages 84–9) and soufflés (pages 78–83). Here are some other ideas.

Cheese sauce

White sauce can be used to make a cheese sauce to mix with pasta for macaroni cheese, or spooned over fish for fish mornay. Take the pan off the heat and stir the cheese into the hot sauce: around 90g/3oz grated Cheddar or Gruyère, or 55g/2oz Parmesan, but the exact amount will depend on the strength of the cheese – taste as you add it, and season well. Half a teaspoon of English mustard will bring out the flavour. Use the sauce straight away or reheat very gently – don't let it boil again, or it will go grainy.

Macaroni cheese

Mix 225g/8oz freshly cooked macaroni with a triple quantity of white sauce mixed with 225g/8oz grated cheese (a mix of Cheddar and Parmesan) and season with salt, pepper and English mustard. Tip into a gratin dish and top with 5 tbsp cheese and 3 tbsp breadcrumbs. Bake at 180°C/350°F/Gas 4 for 40 minutes, until crisp and golden.

Cauliflower cheese

Break a medium cauliflower into florets and steam until tender, not crunchy. Mix 1 quantity of white sauce with a dab of mustard and 55g/2oz grated Cheddar, season and heat gently. Stir in the cauliflower and scrape the mixture into a gratin dish. Scatter over 3 tbsp breadcrumbs and 30g/1oz grated Cheddar. Grill until brown and crisp.

tomato sauce

makes 1 pint/600ml

2 tbsp olive oil

1 carrot, chopped small

1 small onion, peeled and chopped small

1 celery stick, chopped

2lb/900g tomatoes, skinned or a 400g can

a pinch of caster sugar and salt

FRY THE VEGETABLES. Heat the oil in a medium-sized pan and add the carrot, onion and celery. Cook very gently for 10 minutes or so, until soft and just thinking about browning.

CHOP THE TOMATOES. Peel the tomatoes, if they are fresh. Chop them roughly and add to the pan, along with their juice and a pinch each of salt and sugar.

SIMMER GENTLY until the tomatoes are collapsed and melting into their own juices. Purée with a hand blender for a less chunky sauce, and push through a sieve for a perfectly smooth one.

what you need to make a good tomato sauce

TWO THINGS always taste better on holiday: tomatoes and wine. But while that local red that was so good in the Mediterranean sunshine never tastes right in the cold, grey light of a wet British summer, rugged *coeur de boeuf* or marmande tomatoes are worth carrying carefully home. They need the barest minimum to turn them into a sublime fresh sauce, just to be peeled and coarsely chopped, then heated gently with salt, garlic and olive oil and mixed with hot pasta.

But that is a sauce for high summer. For the rest of the year, the deeper flavour of slow-simmered tomatoes makes for a versatile sauce to spread on pizza or mix with little meatballs or use to bind a gratin.

THE TOMATOES

Fresh tomatoes make the best sauce, as long as they are properly ripe. They should be soft and a deep lipstick-red. If they are sagging and splitting a little and are too collapsed for slicing, so much the better. You might even pick some up cheap at the greengrocer's. But if they are as hard as a squash ball and pinkish orange, buy a can instead, which will make a perfectly good sauce, though you can also put under-ripe tomatoes in a bowl on the window sill for a few days to ripen and darken and lose the crispness that is so wrong in a tomato. They will not be as good as a sun-ripened Mediterranean tomato, but worth making into a sauce.

PEELING THE TOMATOES

Bits of skin have an unpleasant texture, so unless the sauce is going to be sieved, you will need to peel the tomatoes by immersing them in a bowl of boiling water and then slipping off the loosened skin. Ignore instructions to plunge the tomatoes in the water for a full minute. If it takes that long to loosen the skin, the tomatoes are under-ripe. The riper the tomato, the less time it will take. Ten seconds should do it, 20 at the most.

THE MIREPOIX

This is a posh name for the chopped carrot, onion and celery, the triumvirate of vegetables that give backbone and roundness of flavour to so many dishes. It is not a disaster if you don't have them, but you will make a better sauce if you use them. Or try the plain sauce below.

THE OLIVE OIL

The olive oil is key to the sauce, partly to soften the mirepoix, but also for the fruity flavour and the body it gives to the texture. Think of it as an ingredient rather than an expedient, and add more oil if it pleases you – the amount I've stated is a minimum. The tomatoes will soak it up. Use an oil with plenty of flavour (I use a fruity, not too peppery Provençal oil) and a flavour that you enjoy.

SEASONING

Salt is necessary to balance the acidity and sweetness of the tomatoes, but add a pinch of sugar, too, to bring out their sweetness. Be circumspect with pepper. If the flavour of the tomatoes seems good already, the pungency and fragrance of pepper may upset the balance.

A VERY USEFUL, VERY SIMPLE SAUCE

An Italian friend gave me this recipe, which is great for simple pasta dishes. Purée a can of tomatoes with a stick blender or in a liquidizer. Pour into a pan, and season with salt, a little caster sugar and a small pinch of bicarbonate of soda. Simmer for 10–20 minutes, until sufficiently thickened, then stir in 1 tbsp olive oil.

good things to add to tomato sauce

❧ Anchovies: a couple of chopped canned anchovies, added to the oil with the mirepoix, will make the sauce richly savoury, not fishy.

❧ Chilli: chopped red chilli gives punch and doesn't have to be burningly hot. A little nip of chilli in just about any tomato sauce-based recipe will make it lively. Chilli sauce is a great quick cheat (Encona is a good brand, with a proper capsicum flavour).

❧ Olives: the black wrinkled ones, sold dry rather than in brine, have the deepest flavour. Reject pitted olives in brine – they have as much flavour as a squash ball.

❧ Basil: this is the classic, but it doesn't do well when heated and the aniseed tones are not for everyone. Finely slice or rip the leaves and scatter over at the last minute.

❧ Capers: add 1–2 tbsp, soaked first in a large bowl of water for 30 minutes if they are salted, or rinsed and squeezed dry if in vinegar, for a delicious piquancy.

hollandaise

serves 6–8

4 large egg yolks
salt
8oz/225g unsalted
  butter, cut into dice
juice of ½ lemon

WHISK THE YOLKS in a bowl with a pinch of salt and 3 tbsp water.

HEAT THE EGGS. Place the bowl over a pan of very gently simmering water (or in a roasting tin, see below) and keep beating until the egg is pale and thick.

ADD THE BUTTER. Drop a cube of butter into the egg and whisk until it is incorporated, then continue with the next cube until it is all used up.

TASTE AND SEASON with salt and lemon juice.

how to make a perfect hollandaise

HOLLANDAISE IS THE BEST sauce to eat with English asparagus, the essential ingredient in eggs Benedict and the perfect partner to simply cooked salmon. It's rich, a treat and a great recipe to have up your sleeve.

Hollandaise has much in common with mayonnaise. Like mayonnaise, it is an emulsion of fat (in this case melted butter rather than oil) with an egg yolk. As with mayonnaise, the danger is that if the butter is added too quickly, the emulsion will break and the sauce will curdle. But there is a further hazard. Because the butter needs to be kept liquid, the sauce must be heated, and if it gets too hot the egg component will solidify and, again, the sauce will curdle.

The most usual way to get round this is to make the hollandaise in a bowl sat over a pan of gently simmering water. There is still a risk of over-heating, though.

The neatest solution, the one I learnt at Leith's School of Food and Wine, is this:
❧ Half fill a deep roasting tin with boiling water.
❧ Sit the tin on the hob, over two rings. Light the back ring.
❧ Put the bowl or a saucepan with the egg yolk in the water at the front of the tin, over the unlit ring. The water at the back will bubble happily, while the water at the front will be hot, but not quite boiling, the perfect temperature for making hollandaise. If the mixture doesnt seem warm enough, move the bowl back a little.

COOKING OUT THE EGG YOLK
The egg yolk needs to be cooked until it is pale and thick, which will take 3 minutes or so, or the sauce will not thicken properly. It also improves the flavour, and should get rid of any bugs.

ADDING THE BUTTER
Classically the butter should be clarified first: that's to say melted, then strained through muslin to rid it of any impurities (chiefly milk solids). The melted butter is then dribbled in gradually, as though making a mayonnaise.

Although clarified butter will make a thicker hollandaise, it's not really necessary to go to the trouble. Good-quality unsalted butter cut into small cubes does very well. It also has the advantage that the butter emulsifies in as it melts. Once each cube has disappeared, it's time to add another one – easy.

KEEPING THE SAUCE WARM

Keep the sauce warm in a water bath or in a vacuum flask but, as with anything, don't hold it for too long because of the risk of bacteria multiplying. A hollandaise can also be reheated, with care, in a pan over a very low heat. Heat it until the sauce slips in the pan (that is, melts just enough to slide around), then whisk it until smooth and heated through.

SAVING A CURDLED SAUCE

As with mayonnaise, curdling is an irritation but not a disaster. If the sauce has split because the butter has been added too quickly, start afresh with a new egg yolk in another bowl. Add the water and then start the whole process again, very gradually beating in the curdled mixture. If the egg has overheated and scrambled, sieve out the solids and add it to a new egg yolk in the same way.

✳ **THINGS TO ADD TO HOLLANDAISE**

➤ The zest and juice of an orange: this is a sauce Maltaise, and is classically made with blood oranges.
➤ Two beaten egg whites: added at the end to make a foaming hollandaise.
➤ Chopped herbs: about 2 tbsp dill or parsley or 1 tbsp tarragon.

MAKING HOLLANDAISE IN THE BLENDER

A last-minute hollandaise can be made in the blender and is a great quick fix. The egg yolks are not cooked out, so it does not have quite the same flavour, and it won't thicken as much, but it hits the right buttons.

Whiz together 3 egg yolks with 1–2 tbsp lemon juice and a fat pinch of salt. With the blender running, trickle in 225g/8oz hot melted butter, stopping before the white curd bits in the butter pan go in. Taste to check the seasoning and use straight away.

A béarnaise

A béarnaise, the classic sauce for steak, is made in the same way as hollandaise but with a reduction of vinegar as the base. Some people like to use the same basis for a hollandaise (without the tarragon stalks), although for me it is too strong for anything except steak.

Boil 2 tbsp white wine vinegar (or wine, if you prefer a gentler flavour), 1 tsp black peppercorns, 1 tsp chopped shallot, the stalks from a small bunch of tarragon and 2 tbsp water until reduced to a total of 2 tbsp. This boiling helps get rid of the harsh acidity and gives a more mellow flavour.

Strain the reduction and add to the egg yolks, along with 1 tbsp water. Whisk as for a hollandaise and add the butter in the same way. Finish by stirring in 1 tbsp chopped tarragon leaves, and seasoning with salt, pepper and a squeeze of lemon juice if necessary.

mayonnaise

*makes a scant
½ pint/270ml*

1 egg yolk

1 tsp smooth Dijon
mustard

juice of half a lemon

salt

about 8fl oz/225ml mild-
flavoured oil

BEAT THE EGG. In a pudding basin or mixing bowl, and using a whisk, lightly beat the egg yolk with the mustard, 1 tsp lemon juice and a fat pinch of salt until smoothly amalgamated.

ADD THE OIL SLOWLY. Beat in a drop of oil, then another, then another. After about a tenth of the oil has been added in this way, you can progress to adding about a teaspoonful each time, beating each one in so that it is well emulsified before adding the next.

NOW GO A BIT MORE QUICKLY. After a good third of the oil has been added, move on to trickling the oil in a thin stream, still beating all the time. If it gets too thick, beat in 1 tsp of lemon juice.

TASTE AND SEASON. When all the oil has been added, taste and adjust the seasoning, adding more lemon juice if necessary. Store, covered, in the fridge.

how to make proper mayonnaise

HOMEMADE MAYONNAISE is a gently flavoured ointment, with a rich smoothness and a buttery translucency. It may seem bland, after the rough sharpness of bottled mayonnaise, but this allows it to work with the food it is served with rather than bludgeon it down.

GENTLY DOES IT

Mayonnaise is an emulsion of oil in water – that's to say the droplets of oil suspended in the water content of egg yolk, plus, usually, lemon juice and mustard. The emulsifiers naturally present in egg yolk, chiefly lecithin, as well as the starches in mustard, act as facilitators, linking the oil and the water together. Just whisking the two together in one go won't work: you'll end up with a curdled mess, not a satiny, cohesive, thick cream. The oil must be added at snail's pace and vigorously beaten to help it break it up into droplets that are small enough to link to the emulsifiers. Add the oil too fast, and the droplets will be too big and the sauce won't emulsify.

Curdling is the most common problem when making mayonnaise. Put a new egg yolk in a clean bowl and start again, very gradually beating in the curdled mixture, as if it were just oil.

To avoid curdling in the first place, make sure that all the ingredients are at room temperature to start with. Add the oil *very* slowly. If it looks like it is about to curdle – you'll soon recognize the rim of oil forming at the edge and the reluctance with which the emulsion absorbs more oil – beat in lemon juice or 1 tbsp hot water.

Counter-intuitively, the more oil that is added, the thicker the mayonnaise becomes. For a thinner mayonnaise, either stop adding oil when the texture seems right, or beat in water to adjust the consistency.

THE OIL

Most cooks agree that using only olive oil makes for a bitter, overpowering flavour. Some insist that all sunflower, or all groundnut, is the answer. I like to have some olive flavour, so I use three-quarters mild olive oil and one-quarter extra virgin. Tasting frequently means I can stop as soon as the taste is well balanced. As for the quantity, an egg yolk can absorb as much as 300ml/½ pint olive oil, but it seems prudent not to push it.

SHARPNESS

Lemon juice can be replaced by good-quality wine vinegar or cider vinegar, but not balsamic vinegar, which will discolour the mayonnaise.

BLENDER MAYONNAISE

Sometimes it is useful to make a quick mayonnaise in a blender or a food processor – one of those miniature food processors is especially good for this.

Use the whole egg, rather than just the yolk, and whiz it together with the mustard, salt and lemon juice. If the food processor is large, you may have to use 2 eggs to get them to mix and double the quantity of oil. With the motor running, very slowly trickle in the oil. Season and adjust the consistency as usual. This kind of mayonnaise is paler (because of the egg white) and less thick than handmade mayonnaise, but it still has a good flavour.

☀ THE EGG AND RAW EGG RISK

Much is made of the risks associated with eating raw eggs, and if these worry you a great deal, then hunt out pasteurised egg yolks, available in some supermarkets. Anyone pregnant or particularly vulnerable to infection should certainly do this, or else resign themselves to bottled mayonnaise.

For the rest of us, some sensible care will reduce the risk a great deal.
❥ Use only Lion Mark eggs, which come from hens vaccinated against salmonella.
❥ Make sure that they are well within their sell by date.
❥ Since the majority of any bugs are on the shell of the egg rather than in it, minimise the contact of the outside of the egg with the yolk, and wash your hands after dealing with the eggs.
❥ Most importantly, keep the mayonnaise, and any dishes containing it, well chilled, and don't keep them out of the fridge for longer than is necessary.

☀ GOOD THINGS TO ADD TO MAYONNAISE

❥ Tartare sauce: mix in 1 tbsp each of chopped gherkins, capers, finely chopped parsley leaves and shallots, and make it sharp with lemon juice. A little chopped tarragon works well too
❥ Saffron mayonnaise: infuse a pinch of saffron threads in 2 tbsp hot water for an hour, then mix in. Fantastic with fish or chicken.
❥ Chilli mayonnaise: stir in a grilled, peeled, deseeded and chopped red chilli, or cheat and use chilli sauce. Good with cold beef.
❥ Red pepper mayonnaise: purée a roasted, peeled red pepper and mix in.
❥ Lemon mayonnaise: add the grated zest of a lemon, serve with dressed crab.
❥ Aioli: mash a fat clove of garlic with a pinch of salt to a purée. Mix with the egg yolk and add the oil. Serve as one of the best summer starters, with a generous platter of raw and lightly cooked vegetables and seafood.

vinaigrette

makes enough to dress a salad for 4–6

1 tbsp vinegar

½ tsp salt

4 tbsp extra virgin olive oil

salt

MIX THE VINEGAR AND SALT until the salt dissolves, either shaking them together in a screw-top jar or whisking together in a bowl.

MIX IN THE OIL. Dip a lettuce leaf in and taste, adding more salt (but not more vinegar) if it needs perking up.

a good dressing

IT'S QUICKER TO WHIP up your own dressing than to rip the fiddly plastic seal off the bottle of ready-made vinaigrette, and your dressing won't have Xanthan gum or emulsifiers or any other ingredients that are there for the expediency of the manufacturer, not the pleasure of the eater. It'll also taste much, much nicer.

THE OIL
The oil must be good and it must be fresh. This is true always, but it is especially true in a salad dressing, where every nuance of the flavour of the ingredients will come through clearly.

Smell the oil. If it has an unpleasant smell, not fruity or peppery or nutty, it's rancid. Throw it away. Nut oils in particular go off especially quickly, so are best stored in the fridge. Olive oil solidifies in the fridge, which is a pain when it comes to cooking, so store it in a dark cupboard, and never, ever keep it by the cooker, where the heat will make it go off more quickly than ever.

EASY DOES IT
There should be just enough vinaigrette to make each salad leaf gleam with thin coat of dressing, but not so much that that there is an oily puddle at the bottom of the bowl, making the last bits of salad drenched. Pour over just enough dressing, then stop. It's better to keep some dressing for the next day, or even throw some away (you'll know to make less next time) than spoil a salad by over-dressing it.

The dressing is there to enhance the salad, not vice versa, so should be adapted to the ingredients. Oil and salt are the key constituents, with a little acidity from vinegar or lemon juice. Dull-tasting dressings need more salt, not more vinegar. In fact, some perfectly ripe Mediterranean tomatoes need no more than a scattering of salt and a dribble of oil.

APPLYING THE DRESSING

Don't pass round undressed salad and a jug of dressing to pour over. All that happens is that some of each leaf will be saturated in dressing, and some will be squeakily undressed. If someone wants their salad naked, let them take some from the bowl first, then pour over the dressing and toss the leaves so that they are all coated. Be sure to use a large enough bowl, one in which the leaves sit a good couple of inches beneath the rim, or it will be impossible to toss them properly. Hands are the best implements, dealing gently and thoroughly with the leaves, but if that appals you, use wooden spoons or salad servers.

Never, ever, dress a green salad until the moment before it is passed around. Even a 5 minute wait can make the leaves slimy and limp.

➤ For a thicker vinaigrette, mix together all the ingredients except the oil. Then drip the oil in slowly, stirring all the time, so that the dressing emulsifies.

GOOD THINGS TO PUT IN A DRESSING

Some salads do benefit from a bit more oomph in the dressing. Most notably, the bitter winter leaves of radicchio and chicory are much improved by a little sweetness – honey or sugar – in the dressing. A warm potato salad is good with the kick of mustard, and perhaps some grated lemon zest.

➤ Nut oils: use all walnut oil or 1 tbsp hazelnut oil mixed with 3 tbsp mild olive oil. Good on a green salad, especially served alongside goat's cheese.

➤ Mustard: smooth mustard gives bite and also helps the dressing form a more stable emulsion, which is good if you want a thicker dressing, perhaps for a chicken or potato salad. Grainy mustard gives texture and a little acidity, so you may need a tablespoonful or so more oil.

➤ Honey: better than sugar, 1 tsp of honey tempers the bitterness of leaves such as chicory or radicchio.

Potatoes with lemon and mustard vinaigrette

Boil 675g/1½lb baby new potatoes in well-salted water. If the skins are at all tough, peel them off as soon as the potatoes are cool enough to handle. To make the dressing, mix together the grated zest of 1 lemon, the juice of ½ lemon, ½ tbsp grain mustard, 6 tbsp olive oil, ½ tsp salt, freshly ground black pepper and chopped fresh dill (optional). Pour over the warm potatoes. Serve warm or cool, but not cold from the fridge. Serves 4–6.

stock

bones

vegetables

herbs and other
flavourings (optional)

ROAST THE BONES, IF NECESSARY. If the bones are raw, roast them in a hot oven for 20 minutes or so, until browned, to add flavour and colour.

PUT THE INGREDIENTS IN A PAN. Put the bones in a large pan and cover with water. Add vegetables and herbs if you have them.

SIMMER. Bring to simmering point, and skim off any scum that comes to the surface. Simmer very, very gently (or the stock will be cloudy) and skim the surface whenever you have a moment. Cook for 3 hours or more, until the stock has a good flavour.

COOL AND STORE. Allow to cool, then strain and store in the fridge.

how to make great stock

THERE IS TIME to make homemade stock; really, there is. I'm not suggesting that one always must use homemade and never reach for a tub of ready-made or a cube – just that making stock is very little trouble and makes a huge difference to the finished dish. So when you have the bones left over from a roast, or the butcher has some going, use them.

It's not just about flavour, although that matters too. Good meat stock has a high level of natural gelatine so it gels when it is chilled. When used in a hot dish, this adds body to it, making soups more mouth-filling and giving a lip-smacking edge of stickiness to a casserole.

IT DOESN'T NEED TO BE COMPLICATED

Chefs make a lot of fuss about stock and it is one of the foundations of restaurant food. But their recipes include fiddly additions like peppercorns tied in muslin and a complicated list of ingredients: hardly the stuff of day-to-day home cooking. Keep it simple and anyone can manage homemade stock. Take the remains of a roast chicken, say, or bones from roast beef or pork, pop them in a pot, cover with water and simmer for 2–3 hours and you'll get an excellent everyday stock. An onion and a stick of celery are good but optional. It would be a shame if stock didn't get made just for the want of an onion.

SLOW COOKERS

The gadget which revolutionized my stock-making habits was the slow cooker. That darling of the 70s and 80s has gone out of fashion, and I admit I rarely use it for anything other than stock (the one exception is cooking the Christmas

GOOD THINGS TO ADD TO STOCK

Do add to stock:
- ❥ Giblets and neck from poultry (not liver).
- ❥ Fennel trimmings.
- ❥ Celery.
- ❥ A carrot: one but no more, unless it's a vegetable stock, or the stock will be over-sweet.
- ❥ Fresh tomatoes: the skins, juices and seeds left over from peeling and deseeding tomatoes are perfect.
- ❥ Onions and shallots: leaving the skins on gives a lovely deep yellow colour to the stock.
- ❥ Unpeeled cloves of garlic.
- ❥ Herbs: a bay leaf, peppercorns, a sprig of thyme and parsley stalks.

Don't add to stock:
- ❥ Liver: it makes the stock murky.
- ❥ Anything from the cabbage family, including broccoli, kale, cauliflower and kohlrabi, since they'll add a rank, sulphurous flavour.
- ❥ Root vegetables (except carrots).
- ❥ Soft herbs such as basil, dill and tarragon.
- ❥ Salt: leave the seasoning for the final dish.

pudding, which it does magnificently). But after a roast chicken or any other roast, I'll chuck the bones in the pot, cover them with boiling water, switch on and go to bed. If I can be bothered, I'll add a few aromatics, celery, onion, a bay leaf, peppercorns. Next morning, there is the reassuringly homespun soupy smell of stock, not exactly Chanel No. 5, but satisfying nonetheless.

STORING THE STOCK
Cool the stock, strain it and store in a tub in the fridge for up to 4 days, or the freezer for up to 6 months. You can boil down the stock to a syrupy reduction and store it in covered ice-cube trays in the freezer to save space.

Fish stock

Fish stock should be made more quickly than other stocks; long simmering gives it a gluey flavour. It's a good idea to add some vegetables to round out the lighter flavour of fish, but they need to be chopped up to maximize their impact in the shorter cooking time. Use white fish bones for fish stock, not bones from salmon or other oily fish like mackerel, herring or sardines.

Chop a stick of celery, a carrot and onion and a bulb of fennel. Put in a large pan with some parsley stalks and about 450g/1lb fish bones (gills removed from the heads if possible, since they can make the stock bitter). Cover with cold water and bring to boiling point. Simmer very gently for 30 minutes or so, skimming off any scum that comes to the surface. Cool and strain.

Vegetable stock

Barny Haughton, the skilful, passionate chef at Bordeaux Quay in Bristol, makes fabulously good vegetable stock. Here's his recipe:

Coarsely chop 4 sticks of celery, 4 carrots, 2 onions, 2 leeks and 1 bulb of fennel. Put in a large saucepan with ½ bulb of garlic, a sprig of thyme and 2 bay leaves. Just cover with cold water. Bring to the boil and then simmer gently for about an hour, skimming off any froth on the surface. Leave to cool completely. Strain. Makes 2 litres/3½ pints of a delicately perfumed but flavoursome stock.

custard

makes 1 1/4 pint/700ml

1 pint/600ml milk

6 egg yolks

4 tbsp caster sugar

1 vanilla pod or 1 tsp vanilla essence

SCALD THE MILK. Heat the milk to scalding, which means not quite boiling up, but with bubbles forming around edge.

BEAT THE EGG YOLKS AND SUGAR. Blend the yolks and sugar together with a fork – just to mix them, not to whisk in air.

POUR THE MILK OVER THE EGGS, beating all the time with a fork. Rinse out the pan and pour the mixture back in.

HEAT THE CUSTARD UNTIL IT THICKENS. Cook over a medium heat, stirring constantly, ideally with a silicone spatula, scraping the sides and base of the pan as you go.

STRAIN. Pour the custard through a sieve into a bowl. There will be little bits of set white (but not yolk) in the sieve – this is a good sign.

how to make real custard

REAL CUSTARD is one of the most delicious of all sauces. The pretender custard powder is nothing more than cornflour, sugar, colour and flavouring. Sad, then, that it should be taken to the nation's heart to the extent that it is as, for many people, the true custard. I might just have to start a Campaign for Real Custard.

WHEN IS IT READY?
The custard mixture should heat evenly to be hotter than you might think: it'll be uncomfortably hot to dip a finger into. It's ready when it thickens noticeably, which it will do quite suddenly, when the temperature reaches the right point. There will be longer glimpses of the base of the pan as you pull the spatula across it. Take the pan off the heat straight away and stir vigorously, still paying special attention to the base and sides.

DO NOT OVERHEAT
The tricky bit of making custard is not overheating it. It shouldn't ever boil, or the proteins in the egg yolk will clump and solidify and you'll be left with a pan of milk and scrambled egg. A teaspoonful of cornflour, mixed to a thin paste with cold milk and stirred in at the beginning, will stabilize the custard so that it can even be simmered gently. But it really isn't necessary, and once you have the knack of making it without cornflour, it's very satisfying.

USING CREAM?

Call me a purist, but a proper English custard shouldn't be made with cream. Using cream makes for a richer French sauce, a crème anglaise. This isn't just pedantry: the limpid quality of a custard made only with milk and egg yolks plus a little sugar and vanilla is just right with the carbohydrate-laden traditional British puds.

THE SCIENCE AND THE SALMONELLA DILEMMA

Undercooked eggs carry a small chance of salmonella, and the risk is increased if the custard is served warm, as this temperature is a perfect breeding ground for bacteria. We are probably talking about the danger growing from tiny to small, but nonetheless it's good practice to minimize it. So cooking the custard to a heat that will kill the salmonella makes sense. Luckily this can be achieved without curdling and overcooking the custard.

Egg white begins to denature (thicken) at 62°C/144°F and coagulates (sets firm) at 65°C/150°F. Salmonella is killed at 60°C/140°F, providing the temperature is maintained for 5 minutes (the higher the temperature, the shorter the time it needs, so 1 minute at 70°C/158°F will suffice). Egg yolk begins to denature at 65°C/150°F and coagulates at 70°C/158°F – and higher than this when mixed with milk and sugar, as it is for custard. So, providing the custard is cooked to the point where the strands of egg white turn opaque, and is held there for 5 minutes, the risk of salmonella should be greatly reduced.

custardy things to make

Crème pâtissèrie

This is useful for filling profiteroles and tarts. Mix 40g/1½oz cornflour with the egg yolks and sugar in the basic recipe, then beat in the hot milk. When smooth, cook over a medium-low heat, whisking constantly, until it boils and thickens (the flour stabilizes the mixture, so it won't split). Cook gently, still whisking, for 2 minutes. Cool and store in the fridge with clingfilm pressed on the surface to stop skin forming.

Crème brûlée

Use 8 egg yolks and double cream instead of milk. Cook until really thick and pour into ramekins. Cover and chill overnight. The next day, dredge with a layer of caster sugar as thick as a penny and blast with a blow torch or under a really hot grill (preheat it for 5 minutes first) until the sugar is melted.

Baked custard

For a firmer set and richer flavour use 4 whole eggs (or, richer still, 4 yolks and 2 whole eggs). Beat the eggs lightly with the hot milk and 4 tbsp sugar plus 1 tsp vanilla sugar or a little grated lemon zest and nutmeg. Bake in a greased dish placed in a baking tin of hot water at 150°C/300°F/Gas 2 for an hour (or individual ramekins for 25–30 minutes). Serve warm or chill in the fridge and serve cold.

index